Character: The Leader's Bloodline

By:

Barry Heads II

To:

Leaders of all kinds. Emerging and current.

*You can't grow muscle—or character—unless you
have something to push back against.*

—Tony Robbins

*A little sin is like being a little pregnant: it will
eventually show itself.*

—Rick Warren

Acknowledgements

It was a privilege to share time with many of the greatest leaders in the world. They allowed me to use their names in completing this work. They form a major portion of the inspiration for this book. In addition, they gave me their patience and time. I would also like to thank my editor LeAnn McCaslin; she labors through my writing. Parker Everhart also added his editorial thoughts to the project. It was a pleasure to speak with those who participated in my survey, and I am thankful for all of the individuals who encouraged me in creating this book. They paved the road for me towards the never-ending journey to greater character. I don't know why I was selected to write a book on character. I don't know if anyone can complete and do an adequate job of such a challenging project. With that said, I give thanks to my creator, God.

<u>**Interviews With:**</u>

-Sec. Leon Panetta, *Former Director of the CIA*

-Ken Farfsing, *Former City Manager—City of Carson*

-Judge Mark Cullers, *California Superior Court*

-Lauren Fine, *Attorney/ Founder—Youth Sentencing & Reentry Project*

-Dr. Joseph Castro, *President—California State University, Fresno*

-Dr. Dayna Bowen Matthew, *Professor & Health Expert*

-Dr. Farnaz Tabaee, *Professor & Improv Guru*

-Michael Grimshaw, *Professor & Angel Investor*

-Dave Berkus, *Business Leader & Angel Investor*

-Anne Miskey, *Former CEO—Downtown Women's Center*

-Rebecca Walton, *Global Tribe*

-Dr. Willard Harley, *Psychologist & Author*

-Joshua Canales, *Pastor—Mission Ebenezer Church*

-Dr. Barry Black, *Chaplain—United States Senate*

-Dr. Sam Chand, *Sam Chand Institute*

Table of Contents

Statistics & Introduction

"What the masses say about leadership"

Question: What do you think is the greatest attribute for a leader to have? Is it intelligence, personal character or working well with others?

INT.= Intelligence
P.C.= Personal character
W.W.= Working well with others

	INT.	P.C.	W.W.	Total
Asian (M)	8	23	19	50
Asian (F)	3	21	26	50
Black (M)	6	23	21	50
Black (F)	8	18	24	50
Hisp./ Latino (M)	11	18	21	50
Hisp./ Latino (F)	4	12	34	50
White (M)	4	21	25	50
White (F)	4	22	24	50
Totals	48	158	194	400
Percentage	12%	39.5%	48.5%	100%
Male	29	85	86	200
Female	19	73	108	200

The general idea of leadership as an adult is very different from the ideas we gather about leadership during our years discovering childhood.

During recess or lunch, children burst toward the schoolyard in hopes of playing with their peers. Within moments, they begin to play a game. Team captains are chosen, and individuals are selected one by one to solidify a team. From what I can recall, no one liked being picked last. And on occasion, some didn't get a chance to participate because they were perceived as not being good enough to compete. This doesn't happen as we age. As an adult, everyone is capable of becoming a leader in some capacity. The decision simply lies in the hands of each individual. Will they accept the challenge? Do they believe they can become an exceptional leader?

In terms of leadership, I was intrigued by the answers I received from the people I spoke with regarding this survey. Some respondents spoke about inspiration, loving the job you do, the ability to predict the future or being a good role model. Others spoke about recruiting the best and the brightest, organizing groups or dealing with various personalities on a team.

Character is the cornerstone in building and maintaining success.

—W. Clement Stone

After a short analysis of the previous chart, it is quite easy to notice the various trends across ethnic and gender lines. Many answers surprised me. When you take into account the differences in pay received by women and the rising awareness of sexual harassment in the workplace, I was quite surprised to listen to the answers of many women. Given, the current times we live in, many women did not count personal character as the most important quality desired for a leader to possess.

Many people voted for the cause of working well with others, and it is an outstanding quality for a leader to have, but great leaders are often compelled to make decisions that do not make everyone around them happy.

It is wise to remember that many of history's greatest leaders did not work well with others. History's greatest leaders actually caused great social dysfunction and uproar during their time on Earth. Martin Luther and Martin Luther King Jr. both went against the social norm while they advanced in their lives and leadership capacities. Were they smart? Of course they were. Did they acquire the ability to lead while getting others to follow and listen to them? Of course they did. But, we must never forget that their leadership caused a great deal of anger, hate and even death threats to be directed toward them. We don't primarily remember these forerunners because of their intellect or their ability to get people to like them; we remember these trailblazers for their character and their spiritual fortitude. For those that actually followed these leaders and worked well with them, the cause for following them was primarily the significance of their personal character. A good working relationship came from established integrity.

Over the course of interviewing hundreds of people, I noticed that some people said they enjoyed being happy at work. They suggested the thought that working well with others allows happiness to flourish during their working hours. To a degree, they are correct. However, no one is happy when a team works well together and the business begins to fall apart. Many organizations collapse due to major character flaws within the leadership ranks. Constant cheating, stealing and a lack of integrity run rampant in organizations that fail. Working well with others is very important for a leader, but solidifying one's personal character is what allows one to establish wonderful work environments with their peers.

As I continued gathering statistics from the public, a smaller percentage of individuals surveyed believed that intelligence is the most important quality for a leader to have. I was quite surprised by the low amount of respondents who selected intelligence. The responses were surprising considering we live in a society that places such a high amount of significance on attaining an education from an elite university, advancing in technology or creating the next exciting consumer product. After taking time to understand their arguments, I obviously came to the conclusion that intelligence was an important quality for a leader to possess.

There are many types of intelligences. A good leader needs emotional intelligence, a solid IQ and worldly intelligence, or what some people like to call street smarts. Intelligence is a large piece of the puzzle for a leader, but it is not the foundational principle for good leadership. I spoke with an officer in a coffee shop about leadership and he made a profound statement on how much credibility he typically gives to a leader with a strong mind. The officer said, "I know some guys with advanced degrees that I wouldn't follow to the bathroom." Overall intelligence and the ability to grow by learning more about one's craft is essential for a leader, but without proper character, their legacy in leadership will be severely tarnished.

Throughout history we've noticed highly intelligent leaders fall from grace. The following story tells of one that was beloved, but failed to strengthen his personal character.

The legend of Joe Paterno was extravagant. He was honored and loved by so many people in America. Joe Paterno had a great personality. He was intelligent, hardworking and he worked well with others. But what ultimately led to his downfall was the lack of strength in his personal character.

My father spoke about this man endlessly during my formative years. His favorite college football team was and still is the Penn State Nittany Lions. With all of this, the facts are the facts. The former Head Coach of the Penn State football team made an enormous error in his personal life. They took down his statue; the entire morale and perception of the institution dropped dramatically. People were fired from their jobs, some went to jail, and many were severely wounded emotionally. This epic downfall was not due to the leader's lack of intelligence, ability to work with others, persistence or organizational structure. Joe Paterno fell from grace because his integrity was in shambles. He did many great things in his life for others, but his legacy and life were destroyed due to his character flaws.

Intelligence and the ability to work well with others are important qualities for a leader to have, but how valuable are Ivy League Degrees or high IQ scores when a leader has a moral failure? What about the ability to form cohesive teams or acquire smaller companies to form a conglomerate? Do these abilities matter if we soon find that the leader has stolen from the company, or presented false financial claims to company shareholders? No, they don't. When the personal character of the leader is dramatically tainted, bizarre issues arise. No one seems to care about their education or friendly smile anymore.

As attorney Lauren Fine has said, "People follow you because of your character. You attract more people to you and they are willing to follow you because of your character."

There should be no wonder why the United States Government is in debt. There should be no wonder why so many marriages in America end in divorce, and there should be no wonder why so many companies are rampant with internal theft. Events similar to these occur because personal character does not top the list of qualities we would like to see in our leaders or in ourselves as a society.

With regard to this project, I conceived the idea at the age of twenty-six. Within a few days, I began to wrestle with the topic and grind away at the task at hand. Some may object to learning from a relatively young individual on the topic of leadership, but age is not the primary concern here. After reading the likes of Marcus Aurelius, James Allen, Nelson Mandela, Margaret Thatcher, Mother Teresa, Gandhi, Moses, Commodus, Cesare Borgia, Khufu and Niccolo Machiavelli, I've gained understanding. I've watched and learned from leaders for quite some time, and I've come to a conclusion. Great leaders are not determined by age, status, birth order, beauty or family name. Our greatest leaders are produced from continuous effort and chiseled personal character.

There is a train of thought that says you're only a leader if someone chooses to follow you. That belief is incorrect. We lead ourselves first, then others follow. Alfred Wegener died thinking he was a failure. The theory he developed is now widely known as plate tectonics, and one rarely finds another who believes he was a fool. Not many followed Mother Teresa to India when she left for Calcutta. She was actually prohibited by her superiors for almost two years before being allowed to serve the poor in India. Who wanted to give to others and sacrifice their life like she did? Initially, not many.

John Maxwell claimed, "Everything rises and falls on leadership." I looked around and saw an enormous lack of great leaders in America. This along with many other questions initiated my search for exceptional leaders. I didn't care what they looked like. Whether they be female or male, Indian or Latino, it didn't matter. I wanted to find the best leaders and investigate their character. I completed my mission, and I found a number of commonalities between these leaders. In the end, I realized that America does have great leaders in business, technology, law, politics, the non-profit sector and the religious arena. We just have to look and observe them intensely.

It seems like a leader falls every month in present-day America or across the world. What are they lacking? It's not proper financial backing, an excellent team, status, fame, well-known mentors or experience. A leader typically falls or is removed from their post because of a flaw in their personal character. The flaw most likely started as a crack, then grew to a breach, then expanded to an insurmountable rupture.

Leadership remains essential in the family, politics, law, education, business, the arts, religion, and in one's own personal improvement. Some question if the issue of leadership can ever be solved, especially in the ever-expanding world we live in today. In my opinion, it can. There are leaders in every field, emerging leaders and leaders already holding positions of status. We will seek to uncover these individuals. Some of the figures ahead are world-renowned, while others are local servant leaders.

I have yet to come to the point of perfecting my character. I find myself committing blunders quite a bit. With this note, I attempt to improve the integrity of my thoughts, actions and intentions on a regular basis. Thus far, it seems to be a lifelong process. Luckily, I had someone start me off on a good path. My father, Barry Heads Sr., was my first role model. He was the first to begin to chip away at the rugged parts of my character. Although he has flaws, I believe he instilled the beginnings of the precious attribute every great leader must have. That quality is personal character.

The word character, in its Greek origin, meant "stamping tool," or "symbol/ imprint on the soul." From that point, it came to mean distinctive mark, feature or trait.

On occasion, we call our character our brand. So, I want you to imagine your brand.

Picture yourself walking into an important business meeting. You greet an office assistant, check in and take a seat. After waiting five minutes and rehearsing possible outcomes of the upcoming meeting in your head, the assistant rises from her seat and approaches you. She looks you in the eyes and gives you a funny stare. You brush off the look and follow her. You both engage in conversation as she leads you down a few long halls. You hear light jazz and see many attending to their work in their offices.

Finally, you arrive at the boardroom. Spotless transparent walls enclose the room, and you see three of the organization's leaders laughing inside. They hold their phones in hand, while pens, legal pads and tablets rest on the beautiful mahogany boardroom table. You thank the assistant for bringing you to the room and enter. After shaking hands, you sit down. Once again, you receive odd looks from the people across from you. Then, you check the "character stamps" on their foreheads. One of the leaders of the company has the word "integrity" stamped on her forehead. The other has the word "reliable" stamped on her forehead. And the final leader has the word

"strength" stamped on his forehead. After seeing
their stamps and smiling, you look into their eyes.
They're all staring at your forehead. What do you
think it says?

One of the more challenging things to
accomplish in one's lifetime is to become a person
of high integrity. In each of the following chapters,
we will examine leaders from a wide array of fields
and backgrounds. As we analyze their words to
extract important lessons and areas of improvement,
we will discover how ignoring these morally sound
principles leads to failure. Through the following
interviews, I internalized a number of common
themes and developed habits that will assist in
improving my personal character. I hope you learn
and grow from these masters as well.

*Ability gets you to the top, but it takes character to
keep you there.*

—John Wooden

Chapter #1

Deal Makers: Politics

(Lessons in Humility)

For through the grace given to me I say to everyone among you not to think more highly of himself than he ought to think;

—Romans 12:3 (NASB)

<u>PANETTA</u>

Secretary Leon Panetta is a pillar in our nation's capital and in the hearts of many of the lives he's touched. His career thus far includes tenures as a United States Congressman, Chief of Staff to the President of the United States, Director of the CIA and Secretary of the Department of Defense. He also served on the Board of Directors for the New York Stock Exchange. Our interview was brief yet powerful.

Our first encounter came as a surprise. He probably doesn't remember. I had a meeting scheduled at the institute he founded with his wife. As usual, I was a bit nervous for the interview, so I asked for the location of the restroom. I was given directions from a very professional member of the office team, then I made my way through a closed door. On the other side of the door, I found the restroom about seven paces away. I also saw a wall full of awards and plaques.

In addition, a solid brick labeled "Geronimo" sat in a raised glass container. Later, Mrs. Panetta would give me a clue as to where this special brick came from. I decided to follow my intrigue and discovered the details regarding this ordinary looking brick. I discovered that the brick was akin to a celebratory plaque for a job well done by Secretary Panetta and the team he led during his tenure with the CIA. The solid brick was taken from Pakistan. It came from the compound of Osama Bin Laden, one of history's most infamous criminals. Coincidentally, standing in front of that wall was Secretary Panetta. For a split second, I froze in front of the restroom door. He nodded, I waved and thankfully, I made it through that interview.

Four years after our initial meeting, I spoke with Secretary Panetta regarding this venture. He was sharp, calm and quiet, yet one could feel the power in his quietness. My first question was as follows, "Why did you desire to become a politician?"

After taking a pause that felt like an eternity, Sec. Panetta delivered his thoughts: "My desire was to get involved in public service. I thought it was important to give back to the country. I am the son of immigrants. I served in the military and recognized that duty to country was extremely important. Then there was a young president that said, ask not what your country can do for you, but what you can do for your country."

After a quick analysis, I was able to peer into the depths of a great political leader. The root cause of his desire to enter the political arena was not fame, fortune, control, or revenge. The primary motive attached to this calling was and still is service. Many people living in North America once believed that leadership in the political arena was a respectable choice in occupation. This viewpoint has shifted because our leaders seem to have forgotten that leadership shouldn't focus primarily on what one can receive, but on what one can give.

As Sec. Panetta expanded his thoughts, not once did he focus his words on himself. Instead, he steered the conversation towards his service to the public. This was a steady theme throughout his interview. One can only come to an intentional thought process like this by becoming and seeing oneself as a humble servant.

The big question is not what am I getting paid here, it's what am I becoming here. Because true happiness is not contained in what you get. It is attained in what you become.

—Jim Rohn

Next, I asked him, "What is your greatest achievement as a leader thus far?"

His answer was clear. "I've enjoyed challenges in all of the public service positions I've had. In Congress, establishing the Monterey Bay National Marine Sanctuary and helping establish CSU Monterey Bay. Providing Medicare benefits for hospice services. When I served as OMB Director and the President's Chief of Staff, the ability to develop tough budgets, that led to balanced budgets in the Federal Government and having a surplus was an accomplishment. In the

CIA, doing the Bin Laden Operation. As Defense Secretary, the ability to develop new strategies for the twenty-first century, and lastly, the ability to open opportunities for everyone to serve in the military."

Once again, I noticed a theme of service and humility. Sec. Panetta never referred to his accomplishments as hard; he called them challenging. This was an eyeopener for me, and it taught me a valuable lesson in terms of how I frame personal goals. In speaking about his accomplishments, Sec. Panetta continued to remain focused on his mission to serve others. He saw the foundation of California State University, Monterey Bay as a method of supporting the educational needs of his community. He saw Medicare benefits as an opportunity to serve the health needs of his community, and he saw the Monterey Bay National Marine Sanctuary as a bridge to promote safe and pristine environments for the public.

Simply put, a humble leader like Mr. Panetta can set daring goals, but achieving the goal is not the primary concern. The people who receive benefits from clearly defined goals are what drives great leaders.

Our conversation continued with the following question; "A few days ago, I was listening to former President Barack Obama speak with Bill and Melinda Gates. He said, 'Most politicians and elected leaders are followers and not leaders. They're called leaders, but most of the time they follow. They see what their constituents care about, then they respond.' My question to you is, how do you get out in front and take a proactive approach?"

Mr. Panetta answered swiftly, "I think you have to be willing to take risks. You have to develop goals and listen to people. . . Leadership by its very nature demands that you have to take risks. And if you're not willing to take risks, you're not going to be a good leader. And I think that's what's lacking. Most elected officials are not willing to take the risk that they should be taking in order to solve problems."

There are a growing number of leaders that are afraid of taking risks. This fear intensifies as leaders focus on themselves. A fearful political leader may remove herself from making a risky decision because it may cause her to lose her seat as an elected official. If removed from her seat, many of the outer privileges of leadership fall away. Business owners no longer return her phone calls promptly, people no longer ask to take pictures with her in public, she no longer has an accompanying staff, and the financial resources received through her elected position cease to flow. With these issues at hand, she backs away from making a risky move. She loses focus on the reason why she was elected. Subsequently, she becomes focused on herself. The opportunity to step forward and become a great leader passes by because she was too afraid of risking the glamour of leadership.

As our interview approached its midway point, I reminded Mr. Panetta about a discussion we had years earlier. "During your time as a congressman, you had a day scheduled specifically to hear the concerns of constituents. This shows that you value people. What were you looking for in those exchanges with constituents?"

"I felt as an elected representative, that you really have to reach out to the people that you serve and give them an opportunity to be able to talk with you and tell you what their concerns are, and whether or not they need your help in some way. That's the responsibility of what an elected official is all about. It's not about him or her; it's about the people that elected the individual and serving their needs."

Secretary Leon Panetta no longer serves as one of the President's closest advisors, he is no longer the Director of the CIA, and he hasn't been elected to Congress in a number of years. With all that said, he is still viewed by many as a leader, and he certainly retains the influence of a leader.

Scenarios like this are not uncommon for exceptional leaders. Due to their humility and focus on the growth and preservation of others, great leaders maintain influence. If great leaders choose

to leave their elected status or are somehow
removed from an appointment, they are still
respected and acknowledged. Their humility,
service and ability to take risk while focusing on the
success of others are qualities that help leave a
legacy for years to come.

<u>FARFSING</u>

Ken Farfsing entered the City of Carson, California as the City Manager of a town in a whirlwind crisis. An investigator was called in to conduct interviews with city employees about harmful activities that were going on in the city. Council meetings were being interrupted with walkouts. Election counting was temporarily stopped, and the former Mayor was legally forced to stay away from City Hall. Many officials pursued restraining orders against the former Mayor. Subsequently, the voters later recalled him.

In addition to the political fallout, the budget for the City of Carson had yet another deficit. The budget deficit was becoming a recurring theme. Eight out of the eleven years prior to Ken Farfsing's presence in Carson, the city faced a budget deficit. There were racial conflicts throughout the city and these conflicts erupted during city council meetings. One meeting included one of the most watched sessions for the council. A statue of Mustafa Kemal Ataturk, the man many believe was responsible for the Armenian Genocide, was brought up for a vote. If passed, a statue of Ataturk would have been placed in the city's Peace Garden. You would think one would call that an ironic situation? Luckily, the measure failed, but the heated debate heightened police presence and the presence of the various government officials at the event raised racial and public tension in Carson that night.

Local residents were also still recovering from tragedies that brought about the presence of Erin Brockovich. The well-known environmental activist spoke before the City Council regarding issues that plagued locals. Many people living in the Carousel Tract received substantial amounts of money from local companies. This was due to the issues of disease caused by companies drilling for oil. The harmful effects of pollution had a great impact on residents.

To top it all off, the multi-billion-dollar entity known as the NFL was in talks with the City of Carson regarding a deal that would allow two NFL football teams to relocate there. The San Diego Chargers and the Oakland Raiders were mulling over the decision. As one would guess, this created a burst of national attention and pushback from residents. Locals, the council, and the business community conversed about restructuring city roads, building plush hotels and creating wild designs for a new NFL stadium.

Unfortunately, neither team decided to settle in Carson permanently, and the council sure didn't assist in courting the NFL.

In stepped Ken Farfsing. He was enjoying life as a newly retired man. He recently retired from his job as the City Manager for the City of Signal Hill. Before he could throw away his work suits, the City of Carson came calling, hoping he would help save the city from its downward spiral. Within his first weeks, he brought remarkable composure and stability to a fractured council and city looking for direction. His accomplishments include being appointed to the position of City Manager for the cities of Carson, Signal Hill and South Pasadena. In addition to holding more than twenty years of experience as a City Manager, Ken Farfsing developed into a well-known water policy expert.

I began our interview with the following question, "You were in retirement. Why would you come out of retirement and take this position?"

"You know, challenge was a part of it. I really believe that cities need to be effectively managed. We all live in cities and we all want them to survive and to thrive. And you have to have good city management to do that. . . Public service was engrained in us as we grew up as kids. My brother was very active in politics. The first candidates I recall as a kid were John Kennedy and Richard Nixon. My brother got involved in Robert Kennedy's campaign. I remember that whole period of turmoil. Obviously, Martin Luther King was assassinated, you had the riots in the 60's and the Vietnam War. So, growing up in that era, I recognized that government was really critical in our lives and you had to have a government that was accountable to its citizens. You need an effective government to help people move forward."

Next I asked, "What are your strengths?" After a quick laugh he suggested the following. "My experience. I have thirty-nine years of experience working in cities. Coming in here, I've had to rely on all thirty-nine years. I also like to network, and I like to learn from other people. I think building a network of the best and the brightest is great for getting you through sticky situations. I'm not afraid to try new things and make mistakes. You tend to learn more from your mistakes than your wins. And I like to give credit to others. When you look at the council, they have to put their ego on the line and they have to put up their own finances on the line when they run."

Leaders have many opportunities to learn from others and share credit, but a great leader searches for opportunities to shine light on those around him. Learning from others and sharing credit seems like the exact opposite of what many leaders in the social arena seek to do. The dominating rule of social and political leaders is to take credit.

Without taking credit, who will know how much I contributed? Where will my applause come from? How will I stay elected?

These thoughts may pass through the humble leader's mind, but they are soon discarded. Grasping tightly for credit or the spotlight soon leads to a leader's end. Those that have helped will soon step away, leaving the one afraid to share credit all alone.

Mr. Farfsing made note of another quality most humble leaders seem to possess. The quality is not simply trying new things, but it includes the accountability that comes with making mistakes and accepting them as your own. Mistakes propel great leaders to success. It's no different from learning how to ride a bicycle as a child. When the training wheels are taken off, the child rolls forward, then falls on his right shoulder. He gets up, gathers himself, then tries again. This time he falls on his left shoulder. He rubs the dirt off his head, brushes the gravel off his forearm, then begins to roll again. Finally, he learns how to balance himself. He rides away smiling, until he crashes. His final lesson is to learn how to brake.

The child's gradual mastering of the bicycle is no different from the training great leaders must undergo to improve the situations of those that follow them. As the leader experiences failure, the cousins of humility spring forth. They are empathy, compassion and patience. The humble leader's experience with failure has the potential to turn him into a great leader. No longer is he extremely harsh, judgmental and demanding. A desire for excellence remains, but it's tempered with the understanding that failures occur and forward progress along with learning are consequences of failure.

As our conversation continued, I asked, "What pitfalls have you tried to avoid?"

Farfsing answered, "We have a code of ethics. So, if the Mayor comes to you and says you can't tell everybody else. This is what I want you to do, but I don't want the council to know. You have to sit the Mayor down and say, 'Look, I have to treat all Councilmembers equally.' That's one I run into all the time. Some Councilmembers don't like other Councilmembers. It's like high school sometimes."

A code of ethics is central to the making of a great leader. As the saying goes, its character that counts. Secretary Panetta seemed to agree with Mr. Farfsing when he spoke about ethical decision making. Sec. Panetta said, "The toughest challenge is between your conscience and what's right and wrong. Whether or not you will be able to enhance your career. That's a tough choice, but I think it's important to always choose what your conscience tells you." Both leaders are in agreement. The benefits of casting away your morals are short, and the effect of decisions like this are disastrous.

Cowards die many times before their deaths;

—William Shakespeare

****

<u>General Studies on Character</u>

Pride goes before destruction, and a haughty spirit before stumbling.

—Proverbs 16:18 (NASB)

False humility comes in many shapes and sizes. If we're not careful, anyone can be bound by the trappings of false humility. I once saw an elected official serving food to locals at a community event. It was wonderful watching an elected official serve residents. I was actually proud to see what was taking place. As time passed, I eventually bumped into the elected official and spoke with him briefly. The first thing out of his mouth was, "Did you see me behind the table handing out food?"

I thought, wow, that completely changed how I view your good act of service.

False humility is dangerous, but losing your integrity runs even deeper.

If a ruler pays attention to falsehood, all his ministers become wicked.

-Proverbs 29:12 (NASB)

The proverb above is a warning to those who believe their small engagement in trading their integrity has no trickle-down effect. Everything the leader does affects her team, from her use of language to her dress code. Every leader has an enormous influence on those they lead. Whether it's that look of uncertainty about layoffs, or the stealing of information from a customer, all actions noticed or unnoticed soon send a current through a leader's team. The leader may not see or feel the shift immediately, but one day, there will come a time when she sees that the supervisors who work alongside her have traded their integrity for the joys of luxury. They have become clones of her.

The first opinion of which one forms of a prince, and of his capability, is by observing the people he has around him. When they are capable and faithful, he may always be considered wise because he has known how to recognize the capable and to keep them faithful. But when they are otherwise, one cannot form a good opinion of him, for the prime error which he made was in choosing them.

—Niccolo Machiavelli

Chapter #2

Lady Justice: The Law

(Persistence)

Let us not become weary in doing good, for at the proper time we will reap a harvest if we do not give up.

—Galatians 6:9 (NIV)

CULLERS

Judge Mark Cullers' persistent walk toward justice didn't begin when he received a black robe and sat on the Superior Court of California in Fresno County. His gradual walk towards justice started many years before he reached the bench. As a child, Judge Cullers' father urged him to play tennis. It allowed his family to become a part of a local club. Initially, the club was hesitant to allow them to join. The resistance came from the racial tension in America at that time. In an effort to break down exclusion policies, Cullers' father objected to the club's resistance. In his own words, his father was sort of a social activist during his time. A persistent walk towards justice runs through the blood of Mark Cullers. With his new course in life, Judge Cullers' favorite athlete became Arthur Ashe. Ashe, known for his ability to win, his graceful character and an aptitude for breaking racial barriers, set a perfect example for many individuals, including a young Mark Cullers, to emulate.

In terms of tennis, Cullers said, "I wasn't a natural talent; I just worked really hard. I just worked hard at being good. I wasn't a natural tennis player like McEnroe."

In order to perfect his skills, Cullers would hit tennis balls against a wall every morning before school for two hours, then again after school. Most students were still asleep in the early morning, but not Judge Cullers. Two hours of practice as the sun rises leaves little time for a shower and breakfast, but somehow, as a teen, he managed to get it done. Eventually, the practice would pay off, leading Cullers to become a high school section champion. His tennis accomplishments didn't stop there. His will to compete continued during his time at UCLA, allowing him to play tennis at the college level.

Standing about six foot six inches tall, Judge Mark Cullers is the most imposing figure of all the leaders interviewed. He even walks with a slight lean sometimes. I don't know if he's trying to avoid hitting his head on a doorpost, or if he's trying to make the majority of us around him feel better about our height by becoming slightly smaller. His educational background includes time studying Political Science with an emphasis in International Relations at UCLA and a law degree from George Washington University Law School in Washington, D.C. Prior to his term as a judge, he served as a federal prosecutor in Fresno, California for twenty-seven years. During his tenure as a prosecutor, he served as the Chief of the US Attorney's Office in Fresno.

Before heading to the bench, Cullers had a bout with the test many law students dread: the bar exam. After asking how many times it took Judge Cullers to pass the Bar Exam, he said, "It took four times."

I replied by saying, "What made you stick it out? Has persistence been a steady theme throughout your career?"

"Well, yes. I think I've always been a persistent person; I've always been a disciplined person. But, I think what made me stick it out was the belief of some people around me. My parents were one thing. But also, my own belief that I knew once I passed I could be a good attorney. So I said, this is just a bump that I need to get over. That's not to say by the third or fourth time I was really getting down on myself and was really getting depressed about it. I definitely had my doubts."

Self-discipline and the ability to persist in the face of immense pressure or difficulty are conditions that create great leaders. Judge Cullers could have quit after his first attempt at passing the bar. He could have taken his massive roadblock as an omen, but he didn't. He just kept moving forward. Even though he may have had unanswered questions about his testing skills, he had no doubt about his ultimate ability as an attorney. His life proves he made the right decision. He now makes decisions that affect people's lives.

Leaders who refuse to persist never reach their potential, and under different circumstances, they're removed from their status as a leader.

I continued our discussion with the following question: "What is one word or phrase that describes your mental attitude during a difficult situation in trial?"

He answered, "Don't panic. Just roll with it. When you panic, adrenaline pumps through your system and you can't think straight. You get scared. If you can't think straight, you can't think your way out of a problem."

Judge Cullers teaches a criminal trial law practice class to law students yearly and this is what he tells his students. "A witness will not say what they're supposed to say, a witness will not show up, a judge will not let you get something into evidence that you believe should be in evidence. Good trial lawyers are the ones that don't panic."

As in the courtroom, so goes life. In our route towards building personal character, or even achieving our set goals, persistence is a key ingredient. With that energizing excitement and struggle toward our goals, Judge Cullers provides valuable advice. It allows one to temper their efforts in persistence. Without a clear mind, persistence will lead to destruction like a runaway train heading for a cliff. A desirable personal quality for any leader is a clear mind, but one doesn't get there without sustaining their personal character.

During our persistent drive toward excellence in business or fundraising, unforeseen issues sprout quickly. As the best trial lawyers would suggest, panicking takes you nowhere. Panicking simply takes everyone in circles. After the first sign of panic, personal fear only grows greater.

I saw a panicked individual up close and personal years ago. I was working as hard as I could in a courtroom for a Public Defender's Office. At the time, I thought I too would be headed to law school, but, luckily, things changed.

As time passed, I was able to handle my duties as an intern. The courtroom was always packed, and there were times when I had to take initiative to help beyond my normal priorities. Jared Jefferson, the attorney I worked alongside, was one of the best attorneys in the office, if not the best. He did the work of three attorneys with the snap of his fingers. He always had a cool head. He had to. On most days, the number of defendants in the courtroom was so high that security had to ask many of the defendants to sit outside the room and wait to be called because there were no seats left to sit in. As I became more efficient, Jared gave me more responsibility. I would make announcements, go into the Judges' chambers and hear the attorneys present their cases to the judge privately and even speak to defendants personally to gather information about their cases. I did this all as an intern. It was great life experience. I had a front row seat in analyzing what a bad decision can do to person's life. It was failure right in front of me. No one has lived a perfect life, but I learned quite a bit during those college days.

One day, Jared missed work. Another attorney showed up. She looked cheerful until she saw the massive amount of attention she would soon receive. She was "on," and the pressure was rising. She got to feel what Jared felt every day of the week. Defendants were angry because they had to come to court. They either missed work or had to get up earlier than they wanted to. They also asked her an array of distracting questions.

In addition, the District Attorney provided his own pressure, and the presiding judge that day seemed like he needed his morning coffee. Considering the fact that I was an intern at that time, other than myself, she had no one to lean on, no one to complain to, or release her stress with. Within a short time, I checked on her.

I said something to the effect of, "Are you okay?"

She said, "I'm fine, I'm fine."

I went back to work, doing all I could to help the people in court that day. Defendants that day received fines, community service hours or jail time. Little did I know, but in a matter of minutes, things would change dramatically. The attorney started to tremble. I saw her hands first, then her entire body. She dropped her manila folders, then walked briskly to a back room out of the public's view. I was surprised. I looked at her, then the judge, then the opposing attorney. They stared at me and I stared right back. The judge called a recess and I went looking for her.

As I walked into the back room, I found her lying on the floor. She was trembling. I was nervous for her and partially worried myself. We couldn't continue; there were no other attorneys from the Public Defender's Office in the room. I quickly called our office, and a supervisor came in due time.

What I learned then, and still attempt to practice now, was exactly what Judge Cullers suggested, don't panic. Don't lose your head. Without a doubt, I didn't want to ridicule her at that time, but if the leader is on the floor, how can a team move forward effectively?

In terms of the mental management of a leader, it's often said that leaders need vision. The leader can have an excellent vision, but without persistence and a cool head under pressure, the vision and the team are going nowhere. We all come in contact with fear, pressure and even insecurity. But don't let it stay.

There will always be someone who doubts you. Don't let that person be you.

—Mel Robbins

Finally, I asked Judge Cullers, "Is there a major flaw you typically find in leaders who have a scandal or fail to reach their potential?"

He said, "Ego. Lawyers have a term called robitis. Attorneys put on the robe and then they have robitis. All of the sudden, they have this sense of power and omniscience. They think they can treat people disrespectfully or bark at people. You have to stay humble no matter what you do in life."

FINE

Young Leader

(Age 35 and under)

Blessed are the poor in spirit, for theirs is the kingdom of heaven. Blessed are those who mourn, for they shall be comforted. Blessed are the gentle, for they shall inherit the earth. Blessed are those who hunger and thirst for righteousness, for they shall be satisfied. Blessed are the merciful, for they shall receive mercy.

—Matthew 5: 3-7 (NASB)

It isn't abnormal to find Lauren Fine working more than eighty hours per week. Graduating from Yale University and earning a law degree from Duke University, Lauren Fine typically finds herself in a sea of unknowns. She spends her hours walking into prisons, looking through cases on her office desk and entering judicial courtrooms. Mrs. Fine works in Philadelphia, Pennsylvania. Coming to an understanding of the social atmosphere in one of the most highly populated cities in the United States can be quite enlightening.

After reading through the book titled *The Ethics of Capital Punishment*, I had a complete shift in thinking about our criminal justice system. In particular, the statistics regarding the use of justice throughout the State of Pennsylvania were staggering. Pennsylvania has one of the highest rates of minorities on death row throughout the country.

During our interview, Lauren added, "You may have come across that we did execute children until 2005 in this country. That's when the Supreme Court said that we could no longer impose the death penalty on children under the age of eighteen. To give you some hard facts really quickly, here in Philadelphia where I work and live, 89% of kids charged as adults, which is the area I focus on the most, are kids of color. That to me is a staggering statistic."

Before her journey into the legal field, Lauren Fine initially learned the art of persistence from her parents and the coaches she trained under as she competed in athletics. She is quite the athlete, playing basketball, track, soccer and squash in high school. In speaking about her potential as an athlete, she was modest, but being able to compete in four sports requires a lot of energy and persistence.

Currently, Lauren Fine is the Co-Director of the Youth Sentencing & Reentry Project. Fine started the Youth Sentencing & Reentry Project alongside a friend who is also a fellow attorney. The organization is a nonprofit supported by grants and financial gifts from individuals. To give to the sacrificial work done in Pennsylvania, go to www.ysrp.org and provide support.

After getting to know each other, I offered the following question. "I'm aware of the time you spent volunteering in prisons during your law school years. Why have you decided to take this venture on full-time? You could work for a big firm, make a lot of money and do this work part-time."

Lauren said, "It's funny, because that's a question that's been asked by my family many times. As you know, the work is not lucrative. So, that creates its own challenges. This is more than a full-time job to me. We wish there were more people alongside of us, and we wish we weren't working eighty hours or more a week. It feels like no matter what we do, we need more time and resources to do what we do, and do it right. And it's not something that I felt should be a part-time gig. It's bigger than a side project. I felt called to do this."

The best way to find yourself is to lose yourself in the service of others.

—Gandhi

Calling is something leaders consistently talk about. They have a constant calling, something that just won't seem to go away. It's quite similar to a flying insect that won't seem to stay away from you. As you recline and relax in your chair, it bumps against your shoulder, hovers over your head or crosses right before your eyes. As usual, you attempt to brush it away. But wait, after moments of relaxation, the insect comes back once again. You brush it away, thinking it's gone, and you begin to relax again. Within seconds, the insect is back one more time, calling for your attention.

The area of leadership one chooses to align with is a calling: a calling to serve, a calling to fix, a calling to learn and a calling to grow. For Lauren Fine, not continuing persistently in her call toward justice would feel, as she said, "unfulfilling."

I asked Mrs. Fine, "You seem to be involved with highly emotional and intense matters on a day-to-day basis. Can you give me one word or phrase that describes the mental attitude you try to maintain as you move forward in your work?"

She said, "I think I would go back to empathy. To see a bigger picture and see yourself in others. . . For me it's hard to answer in one word. It is emotional. In this work, the highs are very high, but the lows are very low as well. We are working with people who, in some cases, their lives are on the line and their freedom is on the line."

After glancing at my notes, I added, "What pitfalls have you tried to avoid?"

"When you lose your morality in service of anything, you're lost. A subset of that is how to speak your mind so you feel that you're not being silenced, but that you're also effective. Sometimes I feel that there is a tension between those two things because there are things we see and that we, in some ways, feel complicit in. Working in a system that is so deeply flawed, racist and oppressive, I wish I could get up and scream and stomp my feet and really just call attention to it. Then there is the tension between our larger goals and what we want to accomplish. We feel that we have to pick our battles and we have to be strategic in the way that we voice concerns and shine light on issues."

Principles are deep, fundamental truths, classic truths, generic common denominators. They are tightly woven threads running with exactness, consistency, beauty, and strength through the fabric of life.

—Steven Covey

The theme of persistence runs through the bloodline of leaders in our present time as well as our past. In addition to Lauren Fine, Mary McCloud Bethune was a leader and one of the greatest women in history. She was resourceful, smart and very persistent in reaching her goals.

Improving the lives of African Americans and women during a time of unrest seemed to be the calling of Bethune. Her pathway to leadership included the political, educational and religious arena. Bethune was the fifteenth child of a family of seventeen children. As one would guess, her family never inherited money in abundance, but this did not prevent Bethune from continuing in the advancement of her leadership potential. After marrying in 1898 and having children, Bethune moved to Florida.

Wielding persistence with one dollar and fifty cents, Bethune opened her school in a cottage home on October 4, 1904. By faith, Bethune built a racially diverse governing school board which included James M. Gamble of the Proctor and Gamble Company. During the first two years, the school enrollment grew to 250 female students. With the support of her advisory board, the school acquired property in 1907 and constructed a building that Bethune named Faith Hall.

In 1923, the school merged with the all-male Cookman Institute of Jacksonville and eventually became Bethune-Cookman College, a four-year, coeducational institution. In keeping with her religious upbringing, students who attended Bethune-Cookman College were required to take two religious courses. Bethune served as the college's president until 1942 and again from 1946-47. [3]

After completing seven years at Scotia Seminary, Bethune headed to Moody Bible Institute in Chicago for two years of missionary training.

Finally, Bethune's influence extended far beyond the establishment of her school. In 1905, she organized a boy's club, and in 1911, she established a hospital. At last, in 1938, she acquired federal funds for a public housing project. She even held a ranking leadership position during President Franklin D. Roosevelt's term in office. [4]

Bethune led in many capacities, and persistence proved to be a steady theme throughout her life and career.

Though they are not identical, Mary McCloud Bethune and Lauren Fine have a few things in common in terms of leadership and standing up for those who are underserved. As our interview concluded, Lauren mentioned, "We as a society are investing more in prisons and retribution than we are in educating children."

Along with her partner, Lauren Fine created The Youth Sentencing & Reentry Project from her mind. They both persisted in generating their idea to form a non-profit, and they persistently seek justice for those who may not receive an acceptable or nonbiased judgement from the courts that uphold the laws of our nation.

Persistence is a key part of every great leader's bloodline.

****

<u>General Studies on Character</u>

For in the way you judge, you will be judged; and by your standard of measure, it will be measured to you. Why do you look at the speck that is in your brother's eye, but do not notice the log that is in your own eye?

—Matthew 7: 2-3 (NASB)

When we think of a courtroom, it signifies class, integrity, brilliance, wisdom and justice. In the minds of many, judges who maintain order in a courtroom serve as pillars for righteousness and justice throughout our nation. We like to think this way, but even judges and brilliant attorneys succumb to moral failure. Beneath certain robes, gaping personal flaws are found. Beneath certain suits and golden cufflinks, we find liars. And beneath shining pearls or a sky-blue blouse, we find a heart of greed.

In many cases judges have been reprimanded for improper conduct. Their behavior was unethical, reckless and saddening. Judges in California have been found to be engaging in sexual intercourse within their chambers. The unethical behavior occurs with court clerks and former students.

With a constant pursuit and persistence towards obtaining justice for others, those who argue and judge the law can find themselves in compromising situations. It unmistakably shows that leaders are human. There must be a consistent monitoring of one's personal character. As Judge Cullers said in our interview, "You can't turn character on and off."

The way in which leaders live their lives and go about making ethical decisions is not always easy. Our character is not similar to a light switch. We can't simply turn on our character when we want to. Personal character becomes habitual. We can turn on a fake smile, act like we're sympathetic to a heated issue or bring about a fake tear. But our personal character can't be hidden. Sooner or later, our character explodes to the surface like lava bursts from a volcano. People will come to find a lack of integrity in our lives if we've repeatedly succumbed to weaknesses in our private lives.

California isn't the only place where misconduct by litigators and judges are found. In Georgia during the early 2000's, a number of judges once gave notice of their resignation from the bench. One judge was arrested for a DUI, another was charged with voter fraud and another was found having sex in a parked car with a public defender.

Misconduct leaves a stain. We will not find perfection in terms of legal justice in any city, state or country. But this type of misconduct, which happens repeatedly, creates a culture of danger. If those who wield the power of the law and hold the future of people's lives in their hands are unethical, the entire system of justice crumbles. Where there is no justice, evil prospers.

The notion that power corrupts absolutely is wrong. We know there are a wide range of judges upholding the law, maintaining court decorum and judging cases fairly. To avoid a tragedy like the many illustrations discussed above, leaders should focus on improving their character. The moment one's character development growth slips, their status of leadership grows unstable and begins to march toward a bone-shuddering collapse

In fact, in studies of how people size up others, morality trumps all other aspects of character in importance. Sure, we take notice if our neighbors seem lazy, but we're especially offended if they seem to lack qualities like honesty, integrity, and trustworthiness.

—Angela Duckworth

Chapter #3

Gifted Minds: Education

(Investments for the future)

<u>CASTRO</u>

While speaking with a man at a cafe located in Los Angeles, I asked him to complete my survey question regarding leadership. As always, I gave him three choices. The choices for the survey were intelligence, personal character and working well with others. He paused and thought for a moment. Then he said, "I think its personal character. You can't be a leader without it. If you don't have character and I can't trust you, what do you have?"

In my opinion, the middle-aged Latino man was correct. After we ended our discussion, I sat down and began to enjoy my bagel. I opened my laptop, added the comment to my survey tally and then thought about my interview with Dr. Joseph Castro.

Dr. Castro is a meek individual. I said meek, not weak. As the cliché goes, he's very down to Earth. He may have been the most tranquil leader I spoke with for this project. He was simply serene. He didn't seem to have an ounce of panic or hurriedness in his body. I don't know if he always maintains his peaceful state, but he's been steady every time I've met him or watched him handle the national media.

As many people in the nation know, Dr. Castro is the President of California State

University, Fresno. He is the 8th President serving the institution and on a short list of minorities serving as the President of a four-year university in America. As the first Latino to serve in this position for the university, President Castro is a leader and a trendsetter.

Fresno State has made a habit of being in the national spotlight over the years for winning NCAA Athletic Championships, promoting academic programs that flourish and for receiving public comments from professors. In every case, President Castro has remained steadfast and has modeled behavior for the entire university and region with great composure.

After taking time to study his background and conversing together, I found that President Castro did not become the peaceful man he is today by accident. He became the way he is by watching the model set forth by his grandparents. He gave special consideration to his grandfather while noting the fact that he served as the model male figure in his life.

President Castro revealed that he kept a watchful eye on his grandfather as he took him along for drives as a youth. Riding along as a passenger, the two would complete a day's work by dropping off beer in the surrounding area. Dr. Castro would watch how his grandfather carried himself, how he spoke to people, how he dealt with conflict, and what caused people to like him. Later on, the time spent with his grandfather would serve as an example for President Castro's future.

As we began our interview, I asked, "What was the purpose behind your desire to become a university president?"

He said, "I think it started with my recognition in college as a student that my life was being transformed by my university experience. I was a first-generation college student, and son of a single mother. I was the first in my family to experience the university education. As I was experiencing that, it dawned on me how important universities are in our society. They are one of those institutions that make a huge difference in people's lives and alter the trajectory of their lives. So, I became curious about universities and I began to study them."

What makes President Castro excellent as a leader in the position he serves in is that he has a connection to the area and the students living there. Since he was educated at an academic institution as a first-generation American and grew up as a child about forty miles from the Fresno State Campus, he is truly connected to the people living there.

Dr. Castro noted that universities alter the trajectory of people lives, and that this significant consideration is what catapulted him into the career he is now in. Sure, the ability to grasp the concept of success and the effect an education from a university can have on your personal life is commendable. But shifting your focus away from your success and generating that same level of passion for others is a truly praiseworthy act, and it manifests as an investment in the next generation.

Dr. Castro acknowledged that seventy percent of the students attending Fresno State are first-generation Americans. This not only solidifies his ability to lead those learning at the institution, but it shows how much of an impact a university can have on an individual's life if they take advantage of all of the opportunities at hand. All one has to do is look at President Castro's current life. He went from working in a fast food restaurant as a teenager to eventually leading a university.

Staying consistent with a focus on student advancement, I asked Dr. Castro, "What pitfalls have you tried to avoid?"

Dr. Castro continued, "I like to use the word temptation. What I've found is that there can be a temptation to choose an easy path. Because of the nature of the work I do now, there are people who have strong opinions. Whether it's a wealthy donor or a legislator or an influential faculty member who might want to try and apply pressure to me to do something that they want me to do. If the leader is not strong, over time they could succumb to those temptations, and I think that's where the character comes in and the integrity. When I have to make a highly contested decision, I go back to what the mission of the organization is. The mission is to boldly educate and empower students for success. And what are our values as an institution. This is my home base when I have to make a decision. The other pitfall is to realize that it's not about me. It's about the people we serve."

President Castro also noted that he hadn't always held this mindset concerning the students he assisted. It can be challenging to find leaders that move forward in their careers by changing their entire mental framework. It's difficult for anyone to do something as radical as this, but it can be done. It's what our best leaders do. Conversely, it's very easy to find leaders who are manipulated by influential donors or highly esteemed peers. Leaders of this type are available in mass stock. But holding the type of mindset President Castro has alluded to is not very common.

In another instance, leaders may promote ideas similar to what President Castro has expressed, but after watching their actions, their smokescreen is quickly revealed. This doesn't simply happen in a university system. This impression can take place in a business or a non-profit. The leader says that they are making decisions with a fierce desire to make every choice have a sustained yet positive effect on those they serve. But what we see are union, non-profit, university or business leaders taking massive pay raises while fees for those they serve rise in the same instance. There comes a time when raises are necessary, but not for the sole profit of the leader.

Dr. Castro's way of thought is essential to becoming a leader who has staying power and the ability to transform others into leaders themselves.

Finally, I asked, "You lead thousands of students each year. What sort of foundation are you trying to lay in their minds for their future?"

"I believe that they're a part of our next generation of leaders. I think the students here know that the focus is on making sure that they're successful and I want them to be very honest with me and all of my colleagues about their experience. They will send me feedback through email, social media and while I'm walking on campus. I appreciate that. Now, that doesn't mean that I will fix their problem. It means that I am aware of the problem, and I can get it into the right hands and have the decision made."

MATTHEW

Dr. Dayna Bowen Matthew is like dynamite when she speaks. You can't turn away from the mind-jarring facts she presents as she speaks with an audience. Her words aren't subtle; neither are they rude. It's truth. Dr. Matthew lays the facts out right before your eyes. Everyone doesn't seem to like the truth when they hear it, and at moments, I'm included in that group.

Listening to Dr. Matthew in a lecture hall at the University of Virginia Law School or speaking with her directly can be uncomfortable. Dr. Matthew isn't a physically or verbally abusive person, what is uncomfortable on many occasions are the subjects she deals with. I once asked her if she felt uncomfortable about the topics she covered. She didn't answer; she just told me it was a good question.

Dr. Matthew speaks about race and healthcare disparities, topics we don't like to discuss as a society, but it takes a leader to push these subjects into the forefront of one's thinking. With her background as a litigator and additional time spent working for the United States Environmental Protection Agency, she stands out as a particularly well-rounded leader.

I began my discussion with Dr. Matthew in a somewhat noteworthy way. Dr. Matthew was sitting in the airport, waiting for a member of her family to arrive in Virginia. What was even more profound was that she was not simply waiting for her family while drinking a latte, listening to music, or reading a book. She was working! As we began our conversation, Dr. Matthew noted that she was working on an academic journal.

After our initial pleasantries and learning of Dr. Matthew's childhood history of growing up in Harlem and Manhattan, regularly attending church services as a child and being committed to her husband who is a heart surgeon, I asked her a number of questions. Thankfully, she was patient and transparent.

One of the first questions I asked was, "What is your greatest achievement as a leader thus far?"

Dr. Matthew stated, "Any student that I've taught and have been able to transfer values of equity, justice and compassion to would be my greatest achievement."

What startled me was that Dr. Matthew didn't speak about the beauty or prestige of being educated at Harvard, or working as a clerk for Judge Thomas on the Virginia Supreme Court. She didn't even speak about her time working in the nation's capital. Instead she focused on the people she'd touched. Not herself. Dr. Matthew relayed messages about her students. She wanted to pass along profound ideals and qualities, ones that led them to care and demand justice for those who may be underrepresented or misrepresented. As she spoke about her students and their effect on society, she said, "That makes me feel like I've achieved something that will last."

As stated earlier, Dr. Matthew's ability to step out of her comfort zone is alluring. It makes people feel uncomfortable, but there seems to be a purpose to her actions. One can frequently find her speaking or writing about the harmful effects racial bias has on society and minority groups at large. So, I asked her, "You seem to be able to quite easily speak about uncomfortable topics. I would like to know how you do that. And if you don't feel completely comfortable talking about these intense topics (healthcare & racial bias) what pushes you out of your comfort zone to do that?"

She reacted with the following, "I have grown more senior in my field; I have had the sense that I have a responsibility to pay back the investment that's been made in me. That pushes me out of my comfort zone. There are people who depended and believed in me as they gave me their best, even if it was a relatively small investment. I went to a very large black Baptist church growing up, and church was a big part of my life. As I went to college and law school, people in my church really believed I could do something for a larger community. Both of my parents died very young. My father died when he was forty-nine and my mother died when she was sixty-one. My father worked four jobs at one point, and they stepped way out of their comfort zone. They sent me to a predominantly white school. I remember my mother trembling when she had to go to parent-teacher meetings. She did that with boldness in order to make sure me and my brother got opportunity. I've traveled widely, and I see more injustice than I care to tolerate, so I've got to get out of my comfort zone the way my mom and dad did."

This professor's words were a lesson learned. She takes the gifts she received as a youth to fuel her passion. I'm sure that fuel is passed to her students on a yearly basis even if they don't know her family history or story. With all of Dr. Matthew's words, she managed to stay focused and didn't seem to take her opportunities for granted. As with her students, the passion she carries has influenced me too.

Though Dr. Matthew's job is to help shape the minds of her students in the realm of higher education, she is deeply spiritual. Many of the leaders interviewed for this book are Jewish, Protestant or Catholic. It wouldn't be odd to include her in the chapter of the book relegated to members of the clergy. Is she a member of the clergy? No, but she seems deeply committed to her spirituality.

While remaining committed to attending church to this day, Dr. Matthew also reads books on spirituality consistently. Thus, when I asked the next question, I wasn't surprised with her answer. "How do you respond to those who say your work is meaningless or a waste?"

Dr. Matthew's fire started to burn. "There are a whole lot of people I wouldn't respond to because I don't care what they think. I answer to an audience of one. If God thinks my work is meaningful, then it's meaningful enough for me. So, every morning I get up and I'm trying desperately. I miss a lot, I miss the mark a lot. But every morning I get up and say Lord please lead me, order my footsteps and if at the end of the day I follow that then my work is meaningful. End of story. But if there are people who say my work isn't meaningful because they are frustrated, disenfranchised and dropping out of the system, I respond to them by trying to reengage and inspire them. There are a lot of young people of color who would say, the system is corrupt. What does it matter? They don't have a historical context of what one vote can do. They don't have a current context of what one vote can do. People say that because they themselves feel powerless. I respond with trying to inspire them."

Dr. Matthew's life seems to be focused and committed to serving and respecting others. This works definitely includes the next generation of

leaders in America and she's done a fine job with
her life's work thus far.

****

T.D. Jakes once said, "You are one idea away from a million-dollar dream."

I think it's critical to add another important philosophy to his spoken word. The idea would be, "Do you have the character to maintain it?" By maintaining it, I mean the proper attitude, forethought, and decision making to abstain from solely thinking about personal gratification. As we have come to notice, leaders have great minds. Many of the world's greatest leaders have been gifted by the creator in terms of their mental abilities, but consistently failing to maintain one's character can lead to an incredible collapse.

Towards the end of my discussion with Dr. Matthew, she turned this philosophy on leadership into reality. I inquired, "Why do you think character in leadership matters? There seems to be so many leaders that get by without it."

Her words followed, "I'm not sure if I want to pass right now, because my thoughts are not clear. I'm very troubled by the misuse of the word character in the Christian Church. Character was supposed to count so much in the 70's, 80's and the 90's when Democrats were in power. The Christian Evangelical Church was so up in arms about Bill

Clinton's character. But when faced with an African American family with high integrity and high character, they ran for the hills. And when faced with a candidate who was three times married, misogynistic, racist and showed very low character, they've endorsed him at every opportunity. So, this phrase of character in leadership is a phrase that I feel very suspicious of. It doesn't matter to many people as much as outcome matters. As much as self-interest matters. I believe it does, but I don't believe it means anything with people who use that phrase often suggest."

A leader's character sets the ultimate pace for a business, city, state or country. The longer the character of leadership is inappropriate, the more damage is done to the institution being led.

A pattern of taking advantage of those one is given the responsibility to support is not only seen in the world of politics, but it also permeates through the field of academia.

When leaders in the field of academia use their influence on students in inappropriate ways, it gives birth to dishonesty and corruption. In addition, it sets a pattern for emerging leaders to follow.

Maintaining one's moral character is a challenging battle throughout adulthood. For professors who have gained prestige, tenure and financial resource, the rules still apply. It seems like a university professor is suspended somewhere in America every six months for a lapse in judgement. And in most cases, it wasn't the first lapse in judgement.

For example, university officials in Southern California have relieved professors from their duties and future employment with respected universities. High profile professors lose their status and financial support due to a lack of restraint. Students acknowledge unwanted sexual advances by their professors, and we view yet another failure in leadership. Instead of assisting in the growth of a new generation of leaders, some professors engage in endorsing the opposite. In many cases, justice is served, but this is not always the case.

In addition, the failure in maintaining an upright standard of morality has continuing effects. The leadership failure creates ripple effects into the institution. The institution loses trust with students and parents to some degree.

In all, there are seeds for the formation of a leadership crisis in every generation. Currently, in America we have an issue. With that said, our efforts should be in line so an ultimate crisis doesn't occur in this generation or the next.

Chapter #4

One of A Kind: The Improv Guru

TABAEE

It happened almost serendipitously. Maybe it was supposed to happen that way. I was sitting in the 1910 Club interviewing Professor Mike Grimshaw (his interview will appear in chapter six.) As I furiously jotted down notes and abstract ideas that came to mind, I saw a woman of average height with relatively long hair hesitate near our table. I glanced at her, then continued to scribble on my pad. She and Professor Grimshaw spoke for a moment, then she sat down a few tables away from us. As Mr. Grimshaw concluded his comments, he suggested I speak with the woman who made a brief comment during our meeting. I thanked him, and we ended our interview.

Dr. Tabaee raised her head and calmly stared me in the eyes as I approached her table. She has a good smile. We started to speak about our backgrounds and why I was in the 1910 Club that day, I expressed my ideas about the project I was working on. As you would guess, this professor, who also teaches improv to budding actors said, "Sit down. Why don't you just interview me right now?"

To my surprise, I sat. Usually, I take one to three weeks to prepare for an interview, but I couldn't say no, could I? So, I sat down, ruffled through my notebook and opened my laptop to find questions and space to record her interview. She smiled and laughed while I eagerly tried to prepare myself to gain wisdom from an expert. What a coincidence, an improvised interview with an improv guru. As she laughed at me, she called our interview divine intervention. I had no time to do research on her background. No time to prepare questions. It was just "Go Time." The whole experience was like lightning in a bottle.

Dr. Farnaz Tabaee was born in Persia. She moved to the United States during her teen years to escape violent wars in Iran. Around the age of sixteen, she enrolled in a Catholic High School in New Jersey. She studied hard while trying to learn English, adjusting to the new rules of a foreign country and learning about a new religion in the United States. She received an engineering degree during her undergraduate studies, but left that field because she wanted to work with people instead of computers. Next, she pursued a Master's Degree, and then received a Ph.D. in Education in Organizational Leadership. Finally, this highly educated woman did post-doctorate work at the University of Florida. As a professor, Dr. Tabaee has taught classes at UCLA and California State University, Dominguez Hills.

Early in our interview, I asked, "Since you're an actress, how do you deal with uncertainty? At times, leaders are very scared or hesitant. So, how should people deal with that?"

She answered, "Sometimes they ignore it. Don't ignore new information or make impulsive decisions. Some leaders research a topic to death, then the opportunity passes. You have to learn how to navigate change and be okay with failure."

I asked, "How do you do that?"

Dr. Tabaee exclaimed, "Improv! Improv teaches you how to do that. In improv, there's no plan. It's unscripted acting. You're constantly dealing with the unexpected, and you can fail miserably all the time. Failure is just data. When you go to the circus and someone falls, what do they do? They get up and celebrate it. I teach people to celebrate their failures. There is no other way to learn. There is no shortcut."

Her thoughts on leadership in the business arena continued, "Information and expertise are all wonderful and powerful, but how do you make decisions when things change suddenly on you and how do you stay present when you're scared? How do you communicate, build teams and do the right thing when you're under pressure and not lose it?"

I asked yet another question to gain insight from her comments. "You keep saying improv, but what is it about improv that teaches you how to handle these things?"

She said, "Improv is acting without a script, but there are certain boundaries that you have to follow in improv. Improv actors have to say, "yes and" as a response to any sort of communication. This makes you really listen to people, deep listening. Then you allow them to influence you. You allow them to change you."

Subsequently, I asked how her statement transferred into the business arena. She said, "If you do improv all the time, you will stop micromanaging people, you will stop trying to control people. You allow them to do what they do best because you're in the present moment, rather than being in the future or past or being scared. For improv to work, you have to listen to one another."

This you know, my beloved brethren. But everyone must be quick to hear, slow to speak and slow to anger;

—James 1:19 (NASB)

From personal experience, I've noticed that most leaders, managers and supervisors don't listen very well. On occasion, I'm also included in this category. Listening, or as Dr. Tabaee suggests, deep listening requires focused attention. This means exerting an enormous amount of attention on someone else. Every day leaders do not do this. They find it difficult to remove their thoughts, feelings, and actions from their primary concerns.

Deep listening is essential to becoming a skillful leader, and without developing this characteristic, a leader will either plateau or begin to decline. Anyone who's led a band, a football team in practice, or a group of kids in a classroom knows that listening is essential to becoming a great leader. The leader knows which section of her band needs more attention through listening. The competent football coach knows his players need to rest by listening with his ears and observing his players with his eyes. The teacher finds creative ways to hold her student's attention by listening to her student's response.

Over time, adept listeners develop a quality critical to becoming a great leader.

Dr. Tabaee continued, "People who can't do improv are people who want a lot of attention, or they don't want to give away their power."

I responded, "What do you mean by that? Giving away your power."

She said, "Because in improv you don't have any power, you just have to be in the moment."

At this point in our interview, we went on a wild ride listening to each other. Dr. Tabaee thought it would be better to show me how to give away my power rather than telling me. She said, "Let's do a little scene." As you would suspect, laughter flowed from my mouth. "So, I say a word, then you say a word, and we'll make up a story. I'll start with Cinderella. It's completely nonsense."

FT: Cinderella.

BH: Grows.

FT: On.

BH: Trees.

FT: Because.

BH: Heaven.

FT: Loves.

BH: Her.

FT: Period.

We both laughed after our improvised skit, then she continued to explain her model for business. "So when you said trees, I could have said, Cinderella doesn't grow on trees. But we made a new story, and if you do that in a business meeting, and someone says, maybe we should solve this problem using open innovation, crowd sourcing. Then someone says that will never work. This person will never talk again. A lot of people won't talk, and women won't talk. But if someone says, let's do crowd sourcing, and the leader says okay, tell me more about that or get more information and get back to me. Now you opened a new way to do business because you didn't shut it down."

We moved forward with our interview with the question, "What is your greatest achievement as a leader thus far?"

"As a consultant, helping companies. I have always kept my integrity and authenticity while helping them be more effective. I haven't taken jobs that I know are unethical. A company might want me to take a job to cover for firing somebody."

"How do you refrain from taking a job when you may receive personal funding or a promotion in your career?"

She said, "I sleep better at night. That's why I don't take those kinds of jobs. It's empathy. I put myself in the position of the person I'm affecting. I think it's the empathy. Money has never been my goal in business."

Dr. Tabaee described her time working as a consultant for a medical device company. The company's ultrasound machine took pictures and transported the images to a computer. Surprisingly, she found that the program had defects. The program misplaced the names of the individual with the accompanying photographs from the ultrasound. With the defects known, the CEO of the company asked Dr. Tabaee to approve the product and send it to the market. He suggested that the project could be improved after it was in the marketplace. The project was extremely lucrative.

Dr. Tabaee responded to the CEO by saying, "No. People are going to be affected by this. I can't put my signature on that."

A good name is to be more desired than great wealth, favor is better than silver and gold.

—Proverbs 22:1 (NASB)

Great people quit unethical jobs. In the end, Dr. Tabaee left the company she was consulting with.

She said, "I burned bridges, I left the company. But that's okay. Who wants to work for somebody like that? Who wants a reference from somebody like that? Whenever I go to a company and tell them no, you don't need me, they've given me another job because they say, she's not just trying to take our money."

Dr. Tabaee's blend of business ethics and uncommon work as a character actor shows the inner workings of leadership. When dealing with uncertainty, risk, or intense pressure, leaders can incorporate this style and create innovative solutions for their team as a whole.

General Studies on Character

Dr. Farnaz Tabaee blends compassion, empathy, integrity and successful communication techniques in her work. These foundational blueprints come from her complex background of engineering, education, improv and business experience.

Leaders like this are forged through many trials. On a basic level, leadership is granted because of a newly required promotion or assignment. In these instances, the influence of the leader only goes so far, and if the leader hasn't grown or isn't en route to becoming a great leader, chaos springs forth.

As the unprepared leader struggles to direct his team towards his goals, his anger catches hold of him. He lashes out at people in an effort to control or coerce them. He may even move to the depths of lying to get his team to do what he demands. Instead of being a great leader, he begins to act like a wailing child, conveniently showing his lack of compassion, empathy, integrity or adeptness in communication.

As with Judas, trading one's morality for money can be tempting. But notable leaders stand

through these tests and reap the rewards of a life
bursting forth with sound personal character.

Chapter #5

Character: For Beginners

(Forgiveness and Trust)

*When you start to lose your temper, remember:
There's nothing manly about rage.*

—Marcus Aurelius

HEADS II

Out of all the leaders I spoke with and the hundreds of people surveyed for this book, no one spoke about forgiveness. Maybe, it was due to a lack of depth in the questions I asked, but forgiveness is a stabilizer for a leader. Leaders who don't forgive turn into hard-hearted, animal-like creatures. They become blinded by their own rage, and their ruthlessness can cause them to die on their own swords. Leaders who don't forgive turn into cynical tyrants, and their paranoia only increases the chances of an impending collapse.

Almost all of the leaders interviewed for this book spoke about empathy, compassion or humility. In addition to the leaders interviewed for this project, many of the individuals who took part in the survey noted in the introduction also brought up the characteristics of empathy and compassion as necessary traits for leaders. None of these traits can flourish in an unforgiving being.

The leader lacking empathy for her team members soon finds her staff doing the bare minimum. While the leader is in sight, employees work hard, but when she is gone, they go back to a state of aloofness and uncaring behavior. It should be no surprise that the team reflects the character of the leader.

Unforgiving leaders have yet another thing in common. The venom they hold stirs privately in their minds. The private stirring typically becomes visible to their inner circle of confidants, then the harsh words and attitudes the leader has grown accustomed to become public knowledge. Knowledgeable leaders refrain from making this a practice. Before speech becomes public, or the leader's inner circle hears of hateful comments, an exceptional leader will allow vile comments to ultimately wash away and maintain a clear and stable mind.

Also, do not take seriously all words which are spoken, so that you will not hear your servant cursing you. For you also have realized that you likewise have many times cursed others.

—Ecclesiastes 7:21-22 (NASB)

Forgiveness allows the leader to move on and be productive. Forgiveness allows a leader to concentrate all of his or her energies toward making themselves and their teams better. The attention placed on a negative comment from a blog, relative, or well-known media journalist typically does nothing but damage to a leader.

Stories on forgiveness are not easily found because it is such a difficult skill to acquire and manage. On many occasions, forgiveness may indeed feel painful to the one who has chosen to forgive. After the initial pain subsides, the gift of freedom is found, and the weight of emotional pain is removed from one's life. As most leaders know, forgiveness is a lifelong spiritual practice.

A common theme found in many of the interviews for this project seems to be that their parents had a great impact on their character. Other than themselves, these leaders found their parents very instrumental in fashioning their character and integrity in their formidable years. This frequent occurrence prompted an opposing thought. Can an individual still become a great leader and have a powerful impact on society while having immoral or less than-stellar-parents during their formidable years? Well, at least one leader I interviewed proved that it's possible. Professor and entrepreneur Michael Grimshaw defied these odds. Despite having had a number of stepfathers, including one in particular who was a famous actor, wise male role models were not a regular occurrence in his life. Michael Grimshaw succeeded as a man and a leader without having great male role models in his home as a youth. The benefits of having great role models that live lives as forgiving individuals is certainly a wonderful gift. However, one can still become a man or woman of integrity while being cared for by those with a less-than-amazing history of forgiving others.

While forgiveness is an essential piece of a great leader's toolbox, the silent killer still lurks inside or just a step away from all leaders. Every leader knows what the silent killer is: internalized rage. As we've come to find year after year, the silent killer releases itself from its temporarily contained status and leaks into homes, bedrooms, offices and elevators.

To avoid internalized rage, leaders must learn to simply let it go. The leader who doesn't forgive others soon finds that he does not forgive himself for mistakes.

Forgiveness doesn't mean a leader becomes best friends with each person they've chosen to forgive. Maybe, the relationship has ended completely, but forgiveness does allow leaders to let go of the past and move into the future with a bundle of passion, freedom and creativity.

With this, the next step is developing trust. No one willingly follows someone they don't trust.

As the leaders of old and those in our current time have found, once trust is broken, the mending process is problematic. Restoring trust is similar to trying to repair an antique with liquid glue. Sometimes, it never is the same again.

In other instances, trust is broken, then is repaired and made new again. What is the difference? Let's analyze it.

From what I can recall, around age sixteen, I played varsity football for San Pedro High School, the quarterback for the undefeated (6-0) Pirates. In a particular rivalry game, I vividly remember running with the ball, avoiding defenders, and finally reaching the end zone. After crossing the goal line for a touchdown, I relaxed. I left myself unprotected for a split second and was hit by an oncoming defender. The hit wasn't overtly illegal, but I did pay a price for it. As I rolled on the ground, I felt a burning sensation in my arm. It felt like it was on fire. Within a few hours, I would find that my right arm was broken.

The ironic part of the entire story is that the hit from the metal helmet that broke my arm was not the most painful part of the process. The most painful part of the healing process was setting my broken arm back in place.

I should have known resetting my arm in place would amount to the worst physical pain I've ever felt when the doctor calmly said, "This is going to hurt." In addition to his short prompting, he brought in another man whose job it was to hold my body down on a table. The man came in so I wouldn't make the problem worse, or yank my arm away from the doctor due to the excruciating pain.

Before setting my arm, the doctor paused, I took three breathes, then I said, "Let's do it." The doctor's assistant held my body down, and I saw nurses running out of my hospital room with agonized facial expressions. This should have been yet another warning for me. Then, my doctor began his work. The pain was immense, my scream was loud and my forearm resembled the letter "L" as my doctor tried to repair the damage done. The process took less than five seconds, but it was absolutely painful. I couldn't think of anything else but pain.

About two months later I came back to the same doctor. He congratulated me on my athletic gifts and answered many of my questions. I do remember a few things he told me during our conversation. He told me that I would be able to feel the weather changes because of the healing process my bones were going through. He was right; I found that I could tell when it was about to rain about a day before the actual rain came. My arm would have an eerie tingle. Lastly, he told me I would probably never break my arm again. He noted that the body would not only heal its broken bone, but it would mend my arm in such a way that it would make it twice as strong as it was before the actual break.

As with my once-broken arm, this is what can happen while repairing trust. The only way my broken bones healed properly was due to the combination of getting my bones aligned, holding them in place and waiting for a definite period of time. To my surprise, what hurt more than actually breaking the bone was setting my mangled arm back in place.

Again, the healing that took place within my body is similar to the healing process that takes place between a leader and his team after trust has been severely shattered. When taking action to rebuild trust, the leader must reset the order of his team. This is often painful. It calls for a clear setting of rules that can be agreed upon, held accordingly, and followed. Resetting the order of an organization can also mean firing someone or reassigning someone to a new position.

The next step for the leader is to create systems for trust to grow ever stronger. With the broken bone, the system was a cast. The cast holds the shattered bones in place and allows time to do its work. For a leader, the systems are numerous, but they must be able to hold all accountable. When one person chooses to become out of alignment, not following the rules, and not being accountable to their partners, trust dwindles again. Finally, the leader must simply wait and allow time to do its invisible work on the culture, personal attitudes and future of the organization.

In many instances, trust is broken due to rage. A leader's rage can be their gift and their curse. Rage used as a gift seeks to end the many forms of injustice in society and causes one to step out and lead. Rage used to end economic unfairness forces a leader to commit to studying and building a vast network of relationships to help eradicate a problem. But the same rage that builds energy in a

leader to come forth and commit to amazing feats is
the same energy that, if left unchecked, can fester
and grow into an out-of-control, burning evil. The
major difference between rage as a gift and a curse
is that rage as a gift becomes bridled and soon
harnessed for good. Human rage functioning as a
curse exploits an emerging leader and places her on
a fast track towards her demise.

General Studies on Character

Trust, forgiveness and controlled anger are all necessary commodities for leaders. The finest leader I've ever heard of is the carpenter from Nazareth. He was able to build trust that still lingers on to this day. He has billions of followers who are currently living or have passed on. Many of His followers have lived an abundant life by following His words. He displayed forgiveness throughout His leadership and His ability to control outward expressions of anger for proper use contributed to His leadership stature.

The parable found in the eighteenth chapter of Matthew shows the eventual demise of leaders who don't acquire the gifts of trust, forgiveness and bridled anger.

"For this reason the kingdom of heaven may be compared to a king who wished to settle accounts with his slaves. When he had begun to settle them, one who owed him ten thousand talents was brought to him. But since he did not have the means to repay, his lord commanded him to be sold, along with his wife and children and all that he had, and repayment to be made. So the slave fell to the ground and prostrated himself before him, saying,

'Have patience with me and I will repay you everything.'

"And the lord of that slave felt compassion and released him and forgave him the debt. But that slave went out and found one of his fellow slaves who owed him a hundred denarii; and he seized him and began to choke him, saying, 'Pay back what you owe.' So his fellow slave fell to the ground and began to plead with him, saying, 'Have patience with me and I will repay you.' But he was unwilling and went and threw him in prison until he should pay back what was owed."

"So when his fellow slaves saw what had happened, they were deeply grieved and came and reported to their lord all that had happened. Then summoning him, his lord said to him, 'You wicked slave, I forgave you all that debt because you pleaded with me. Should you not also have had mercy on your fellow slave, in the same way that I had mercy on you?' And his lord, moved with anger, handed him over to the torturers until he should repay all that was owed him."

Chapter #6

The Money Makers: Business

(Integrity)

Integrity. The sine qua non. That is what I listen for first when I meet any company founder, and if I don't get an internal reading that the entrepreneur is completely forthright and square, I don't go further, no matter how much potential I see in the company. Period.

—David Rose

Berkus

*Regardless of your position, industry, or where you
might fall on an org chart, if you want to become a
world class leader, you must realize that the only
way you can reach your potential is to first help
your team achieve theirs.*

—Brian Souza

Dave Berkus should be called coach. In the
field of business, he is an absolute winner. His
experience as an investor is broad. He's made over
one hundred and seventy-six first time investments
and over one hundred and thirty-six second time
investments in various companies.

Dave Berkus began his journey towards his
current status during his adolescent years. Mr.
Berkus was raised in a family in which working for
yourself was the norm. This history of
entrepreneurship began with his grandfather. As he
stated, "My family has been my model going back
to my grandfather and I remember none of my
family members had ever worked for somebody
else. They all created businesses and worked for
themselves. It was expected. When I created my
first business at the age of fifteen, it was a
phonograph record business. I worked out of my
bedroom. Then later on, I created tapes for schools,
colleges (USC, UCLA, Stanford) and churches."

The business Dave began at age fifteen endured for many years. Subsequently, Dave ran the business for a total of nineteen years. Yes, the business he began as a teen endured for more than a decade.

With great persistence and success in his first business, Dave began starting more companies and eventually launched his coaching career. It must be noted that with all of his success, Mr. Berkus did not seem like an arrogant man when I spoke with him. He's donated large sums of money to a university, and he's also donated a third of his money to non-profits. How many people in your life do you know that can honestly say they do the equivalent with their money?

The average American gives less than ten percent of their yearly income away. Thus, this type of giving is truly incredible. To give a third of your personal income away is simply astounding and shows that Dave's goal in business is not to simply serve himself. Giving with this sort of extravagance shows how integrity flows throughout the entire framework of an exceptional leader. Someone may say, "Dave can give this amount of money away because he's a wealthy man." I would counter and say he is a wealthy man because he is giving his money away. He's not solely focusing on himself, and giving has brought a return for himself and his family.

Once more, Dave Berkus seemed nothing like an arrogant man during our conversation. As one would expect, in the current phase of his career, Dave serves as a public speaker, and he frequently speaks about one of his more humbling experiences. As an angel investor, Dave was given a pitch about a small, yet thrilling company. He was asked to give an initial investment of $100,000 dollars toward the small company. When asked to give the initial investment, he debated the issue of not wanting to fly his plane over a thousand miles to go to a company and help a young CEO named Jeff Bezos. Thus, he decided to turn down the opportunity to invest in the small company called Amazon. The no-name leader eventually turned into one of the richest men in the world. Dave's initial $100,000 dollar investment would have grown to more than eighteen $18,000,000,000 dollars today. Mr. Berkus laughs about the event now, but it has helped him remain humble as an investor and businessman.

As a leader, Dave ventured into the computer-programming world. At one point, Mr. Berkus led a group of more than 200 employees in generating 16% of the world's automated hotels. Yes, that's right, 16% of the automated hotels in the world. He sold the business in 1993 and ventured into his life as a coach.

As a coach, Dave learned that, "Success is based upon the people you hire, train and let go." A full 10% of all of the members of the automated

hotel hall of fame came from his company. Dave
has shown his integrity by allowing people to step
away from his companies. The thinking behind this
is to allow former workers to reach their potential.
Sometimes that means allowing productive workers
to grow elsewhere. Instead of attempting to prevent
workers from leaving and hoarding talent for
himself, Mr. Berkus shows his character by seeking
the best for his employees.

With all of his wins, Dave said, "If you can't
live with yourself, then there is no reason to do all
of this. It has been a joy to see other people
succeed. There is no way in the world I would have
wanted to succeed on the back of someone else as
opposed to succeeding with someone else."

Integrity is the state of being whole and
undivided. Only a happy, secure and joyful person
can seek to serve others in their full capacity.

Towards the end of our conversation, I
asked Dave, "What is one attribute leaders need to
lead others in an excellent fashion?"

He said, "Subordinating their own ego. To
understand that your success is based upon the
people that you hire, and second, that you train, and
third, that you let loose when necessary. Servant
leadership allows you to grow by selection and
training of others that are as good or better than you
are."

Integrity for those seeking to rise in business doesn't simply concern one's intentions with money, but it has a great deal to do with how one chooses to deal with people.

Training someone better than yourself not only relieves you of the destructive nature of pride, but it is quite humbling. Handling the funds a business acquires with integrity is necessary, but treating yourself and others with integrity may be even more important.

The leader who treats a team with integrity gives her utmost to those she's decided to train. She doesn't hold back wisdom or shortchange her team for fear that someone may eclipse their status. Why would a secure leader do that? Whenever this is done, team members are not the only individuals that suffer, but the leader suffers as well. Maybe not outwardly, but inwardly. They suffer in their conscience. In their conscience fear arises and the knowing that they did not do their best in preparing another when the opportunity was present.

After twenty years of studying millionaires across a wide spectrum of industries, we have concluded that the character of the business owner is more important in predicting his level of wealth than the classification of his business.

—Stanley Thomas

Grimshaw

*We value people most who have what I call the
three C's: character, common sense, and creativity.*

—Ray Dalio

We met in the 1910 Club at California State
University, Dominguez Hills for our interview. I got
there a bit early since I didn't know where the 1910
Club was located. I was familiar with the university,
but not this restaurant located on the campus in
particular. Meeting Professor Michael Grimshaw
was sort of a full-circle moment for me.

As a child, my father coached basketball for
the Toros, thus, I was quite familiar with the
campus, its culture and the type of people that
frequented it. As I got myself adjusted, removing
my pen, pad and recorder from my carrier, I was
well aware of my time as an adolescent playing
basketball in the gym, watching my father coach
collegiate athletes and recording practice as a
twelve-year-old.

In due time, Professor Grimshaw entered the
1910 Club. He was happy and recognized me
almost immediately. When he finally arrived at the
table where I was seated, he dropped his briefcase,
peered toward the adjacent television screen and
noticed the President's newly sworn official
government appointee speaking to the American

public. To put it lightly, he looked bewildered, then he protested, "We can't keep doing this."

We noticed yet another appointee to the President's administration in 2017. As you now know, Professor Grimshaw is funny and a bit sarcastic. On multiple occasions, he called me his stalker (it was quite funny), and he even paid for dinner. He directly asked me if I had a budget for our meeting and I sat briefly silent. I intended to pay for our meals, but he insisted. I had a chicken quesadilla and he had a burger. The meal wasn't too expensive, but it was most likely pennies for the former president of a local angel investment group.

As a businessman, Michael Grimshaw's resume is quite impressive. After serving in Vietnam and attending California State University, Northridge, Mr. Grimshaw moved to the Silicon Valley to jumpstart his career. He worked as a business owner, coach, consultant, angel investor and college professor teaching at multiple universities.

As one would guess, with this extensive background, Michael Grimshaw has an abundance of energy. In 2000, he semi-retired from the Silicon Valley and settled full-time in Southern California. Locals call it the South Bay Region. About a decade into retirement, Mr. Grimshaw got the itch to serve our world once again. He began meeting with three local university presidents, and eventually, spearheaded a competition for business students at the various universities. With this, he began teaching college courses in mathematics and business and launched his teaching career in the university system.

After hearing of his adventures in the Silicon Valley during the "Gold Rush Era," and learning about the extravagant financial deals that were constructed every day in restaurants like the one we sat in, I launched into our reason for meeting. One of my initial questions to this guru was, "Why did you become a teacher and why are you interested in entrepreneurship?"

It took very little time for him to answer, "Because that's where you make the money and it's the most fun. Average income for an entrepreneur in the United States is $170,000. Those are small business owners, those are people who have been in business for many years. Now, I would not say Amazon and Google are entrepreneurial companies anymore. They aren't start-up companies anymore. They were at one point. I think on average, about 15% of the population are entrepreneurs."

I continued, "Why is it so hard to be an entrepreneur?"

"Because you are your own worst enemy. Fear, uncertainty and doubt in your mind will keep you from doing anything that is out of the ordinary. It's like any skill. If you practice it, you will become good at it. And you will never go back. You will never go have a job somewhere."

In that moment, I thought through Professor Grimshaw's statements. He wasn't the typical college professor. He didn't just study business; he actually lived it in the Silicon Valley, as an angel investor, as a consultant and as a coach. He has knowledge, experience and the confidence to endorse his thoughts.

A job is not a terrible thing to have, but I understood Mr. Grimshaw's point. Many of us have the ability to fly and succeed in a greater fashion than we know, but we won't try because of the gut-wrenching fear that accommodates dreams, goals and the inherent desire for more.

...thoughts of fear, doubt and indecision crystallize into weak, unmanly, and irresolute habits, which solidify into circumstances of failure, indigence, and slavish dependence...

—James Allen

Mr. Grimshaw not only spoke about fear, but he talked about money. The green nylon that everyone wants to acquire, but few like to talk about openly and honestly. He noted that what he did was fun.

How many people say their job is fun? We typically hear words like, "grueling," "arduous," "I can't wait to hit the lottery," or "I'm here for my kids." Of course, the last excuse is commendable, but not authentically courageous if one really tries to make the most of themselves over the long-term.

Making money can be fun, but it is where our integrity is challenged the most on many occasions. Green nylon tugs at the hearts and minds of many of those living in America. And why shouldn't it? It is what we use to eat and live in safe, yet comfortable surroundings. It is what we use to send our children to challenging institutions for higher learning, and it is what is used to gratify our pleasures. Money is basic to living in today's world.

While money is crucial to modern life, it should be noted that acquiring money can be exciting. The avenues one takes in obtaining it are even more important to the inner peace and longevity one receives after developing the abilities to obtain large sums of it.

Gaining money in haste, without economic or moral integrity is disastrous. In due time, the money leaves and you're stuck with a battered conscience that thrashes at your mind and soul. It's quite pitiful. Yes, making money may bring great thrills, but that won't last. Attempting to have money endure by obtaining it without integrity is like you trying to beat Usain Bolt in the 100-meter dash while you're running backwards.

The integrity we should all strive for in connection with our modern mode of currency is to give it away. It may seem odd, but giving money away re-energizes you, not only spiritually, but physically. When we give our money away wisely, we see it produce. One who gives their money away to people or assist those in other countries see their gifts multiply by bringing farming assistance or education to those living in underprivileged areas.

Giving also allows the financial current to continue. As Jim Rohn said, "Giving starts the receiving process." If you don't believe it, think about what you do naturally. Yes, I'm speaking with regard to your breathing. You give, then you receive. You exhale, then you inhale. You release carbon dioxide, then you inhale oxygen. If you don't release, then you won't receive. It's very simple. We even see this concept in nature.

As we continued our interview I asked, "Other than yourself, who helped form your character most?"

He responded, "Personally, I never knew my dad. I never met him. And my mom was married a number of times. She died at fifty. So, I never really had a man in my life. Someone to guide me or coach me to what manhood was like. The closest was a stepfather I had. He was a famous actor, a character actor. I probably felt the closest to him. I got in trouble with the law early on and he helped me. He was not a great role model, he was an alcoholic, smoked like crazy and had a number of wives. But he took me in as his son right away, and I found that he listened to me and understood me most. And my mom, she was my guiding light."

Michael Grimshaw wasn't born with a silver spoon in his mouth. His father wasn't a billionaire and his mother didn't own multiple clothing establishments, but he found a way to live a life of integrity while becoming financially productive. He shares a bond with a few of the leaders interviewed in this book. The bond deals with those who did not have a steady father figure as they matured through their childhood years. After expressing himself and making note of the fact that he had a bit of a troubled childhood, he made no excuses. He did not complain, and he did not seem despondent. Like many leaders living today, he was an outcome of years of refined character growth. Living a life and handling his business affairs made him what he was in that moment. Sitting before me was a man who'd become a college professor, notable member of the local community, established individual in trade and even a respected consultant. One doesn't earn those levels of status without the accumulated years of effort and resolve in defining their integrity. What they will be? Who they will become, and what they will stand for?

What I may have liked most about Mr. Grimshaw is that he spoke directly. From my time being around him, he was not full of games. He spoke about those who have nurtured their integrity and those who have little to no integrity. For example, I asked him, "Why do you think character in leadership matters?"

He said, "Because we don't have any. It's not all about what's in my pocketbook. We're all here for a certain amount of time and it's our responsibility to do our best with it."

As Mr. Grimshaw ate his burger and showed me a few of the books he was reading in his spare time, I asked, "What is your greatest achievement as a leader thus far?"

After a moment of deep thought, he spoke. "If I can take 5-10% of these students and change their life into a direction that will be more beneficial for them as they go forward, then that is my greatest achievement."

As you would guess, Professor Grimshaw's interview had highlights. None other than the following. I inquired, "Have there been any pitfalls that you've tried to avoid?"

His answer, "Ignorant, stupid and lazy people."

The beginning of wisdom is: Acquire wisdom; And with all of your acquiring, get understanding.

—Proverbs 4:7 (NASB)

General Studies on Character

Today, the leaders in the industry of business don't always walk the line of integrity. People cry out against small payday loan companies and call them sharks against the poor. Local car salesmen who sell cheap or used cars receive dirty looks for their interest in their line of work. But what many fail to realize at times is that corruption or the loss of integrity doesn't simply happen in small place; corruption can happen with large companies that seem to prosper and help people across America.

In 2017, one of the nation's largest businesses which provides workout facilities for the public paid $1.2 million in civil penalties, plus restitution to members, for claims that it falsely promised low annual renewal rates to members in exchange for large up-front membership fees.

The trouble appeared to start in 2006, when the company changed its membership contract to allow for annual rate increases—but sales representatives allegedly continued to promise consumers between 2006 and 2009 that their rates would remain low. In 2015, the organization began to hike rates for some members, who felt that those verbal agreements were violated.

Estimated were that rates of at least 100,000 members were raised in 2015, but it was unclear how many of them were promised lower rates. The company had about 4 million members. [2]

Whether one plays the role of the "small or big" business owner or salesman, personal character matters. And as many workers come to realize, the character of the leader infiltrates the cells of the entire organization. Without an in-depth look into the actions of those leading an organization, a collapse will occur. The breakdown may occur within six months, a year or even decades down the road. But one can be sure that a crisis will occur, and public disgrace will come in due time.

Be more concerned with your character than your reputation because character is what you really are, while your reputation is merely what others think you are.

—John Wooden

Chapter #7

The Fixer: Marriage Connections

(Faithfulness)

Harley

Is love sustainable? Many groups in society find it impossible to sustain a feeling of intense passion and love in marriage. They've come to find that love fluctuates. Unfortunately, people find themselves on a never-ending mission and ride from person to person grasping for intense feelings, then leaving once the intensity of a new relationship subsides. They believe that humans grow and change, along with the passing feeling of love. They find love similar to the fleeting vapors that rise from metal pots as they rest on hot stoves.

When speaking of romantic love, Dr. Willard "Bill" Harley has come to the conclusion that romantic love is sustainable. Others would fiercely disagree, especially many of the divorcees living on earth today. As the dreadful statistics on those choosing not to get married and those getting divorced rise, Dr. Harley stands as one of the few that believes he can not only stimulate but can keep romantic love alive throughout the duration of a marriage.

As a youth, Dr. Harley should have known he would soon create a lasting pathway towards becoming a licensed counselor. Practicing in the field of psychology runs through his veins. Dr. Harley's father was a psychologist, but he avoided the callings for a definite period of time. As a child, he actually thought psychology was witchcraft. Then, his conversion with the unknown began.

Like all leaders, something quite startling continued to occur in Dr. Harley's early adult years. As he states, "People kept coming to me with their problems." Those problems were marital problems to be exact. This is one of the inevitable facets of becoming a leader, dealing with problems. Here started the beginning of a new phase in Dr. Harley's life.

Before his merge into the field of psychology, Dr. Harley studied artificial intelligence. Many of his reading habits began in college, and Dr. Harley still reads Science America to this day. He hasn't missed reading an issue of Science America since his days in college as an undergraduate student. After celebrating the victory of earning a college degree, Dr. Harley went on to obtain a Ph.D. in Psychology from the University of California, Santa Barbara.

After obtaining his degrees, Dr. Harley moved with his wife to Minnesota, where he went on to found thirty-four mental health clinics within the State. At one point, he served as the director of the largest network of mental health clinics in Minnesota. With his decades of experience working with married couples, and the more than fifty years of being married to his wife, Dr. Willard Harley has quite a bit to say on the subject of romance between men and women hoping to maintain their union in marriage.

In addition, after more than a decade of counseling couples, Dr. Harley wrote his famous book, *His Needs, Her Needs*, which went on to sell more than four million copies. He has written a number of books on the topic of marriage, and continues to be influential through his website, Marriage Builders. His work specifically focuses on intimate relationships between one man and one woman.

For a number of reasons, divorce is an issue in all societies. Not only does it hurt the two adults divorcing mentally and emotionally, but divorce provides very little positive reinforcement for children. Of course, there is an exception to this rule, but extreme cases are not the norm. Divorce has an enormous drain on the economy and the financial burden of those enduring it. Finally, families, friends, and neighbors also have to face the wrathful vengeance of a divorce.

One might say, "What does marriage have to do with leadership?" Whether the person is male or female, their marriage has nothing to do with their work as a leader in the workplace. The marital union is private, and our work is public. But this theory couldn't be further from the truth. Choosing a marriage partner is one of the top three to five decisions an individual makes in his or her life.

Whether they are male or female, repeated acts of unfaithfulness to their partner will drain and damage their potential of excelling to their highest ability in their careers.

Quite a number of people seem to believe that one's faithfulness in marriage is not connected with their effectiveness as a leader. Once again, I would disagree. If an individual chooses not to be kind, forgiving, faithful and respectful to a person they've chosen to merge their entire life with, then do you really think they will be able to lead groups of people to the best of their abilities? Is it possible? No, it's not.

If the government identifies a man and woman as one entity, they move on to sign a legal document stating their union, they create new human beings together and they rest at night together in the same bed, there is an extraordinary merging taking place. These two individuals not only sign a contract making their union official, but they eat meals on an almost daily basis together as well. With all of these changes, if they are unable to remain faithful to each other, something must change.

Do you really believe that a leader not behaving in a faithful, loving and respectable manner with their spouse is going to behave in an orderly way with you as a follower or employee? It's hard to fathom, but if someone will take advantage of their spouse repeatedly, then they will definitely take advantage of someone who is dependent on their decisions as a leader.

I held this frame of mind as I asked Dr. Harley a number of questions.

Dr. Harley doesn't avoid hard questions. His life is spent dealing with difficult questions, questions that can ultimately have a large impact on someone's mind, body and soul. Marriage counselors like Dr. Harley have decades of experience listening and attempting to fix marriages that have fallen into deep ruts.

After about twenty-five minutes of interviewing Dr. Harley, I asked the following question: "Is there a major flaw you typically find in leaders who have a scandal or fail to reach their potential?"

He said, "I'd say one of the greatest flaws is infidelity."

I quickly blurted out, "Why did you say that?"

He said, "Infidelity is a huge scourge. When you cheat on your spouse, you cheat on God. It is a gigantic sin. And in politics, it's seen everywhere. I am a counselor who counsels politicians, and they are basically having affairs right and left. And I think it's a huge drag on their happiness, effectiveness, and on their life. People who have a genuinely good marriage tend to be great politicians. But there are very few people who do that. There are a lot of cheaters out there."

Dr. Harley's words don't simply apply to those who craft the laws the citizens of the United States live by, but his words apply to leaders everywhere. Infidelity causes a leader to lose his or her focus, passion and energy. It should be noted that no one living on earth today is perfect, and God forgives acts of adultery from a humble and contrite soul, but cheating on one's spouse should be avoided at all cost. For future leaders that are currently in an emerging state, Dr. Harley's words are a source of great caution and all should take heed of his wisdom.

I continued with my questions. "What percentage of politicians would you say cheat on their spouses? I know you don't have stats in front of you, but give an estimate."

He declared, "I would say way over 50%. 70% maybe."

I continued, "How does infidelity hurt a politician's effectiveness?"

Dr. Harley took a deep breath, then continued with his thoughts, "Well, first of all, they have to be dishonest. They have to have a secret second life and they have to lie about things. They can be easily manipulated. People can say, I know about your relationships, I want you to vote for my bill. There is just nothing good about an affair. I think what we're finding with technology in this country is that there will be fewer and fewer affairs."

I am not married, and I am not a marriage expert. But I've spoken to one, and I've seen the effects of infidelity like many of you have. Infidelity can wreck a house, a family, a business, a city or a country. A leader's vigilance in this area serves as one of the greatest barriers to losing their leadership influence, ability and status.

Dr. Harley is no different from many of the leaders interviewed for this book. He expressed his interest in government and also noted that he was once a lobbyist for marital issues on the State level while living in Minnesota.

Dr. Harley revealed a noteworthy example of a leader who faced massive problems due to his habits with infidelity. While lobbying government leaders with regard to a tort, Dr. Harley suggested that he wanted to help push forward a legislative bill that would give a spouse that's been cheated on the ability to sue the individual that their former partner was having an affair with.

As one would guess, political leaders were on either side of the political line. The Democrats were on one side and the Republicans were on another. While lobbying, Dr. Harley asked a political leader, "Do you think your wife has the right to have an affair? The man said absolutely. Then I said, do you think that she feels you have the right to have an affair? The politician said, I don't know, I should ask her."

Whether you agree with the law or not is not the issue. The issue is that Dr. Harley was speaking to a man who was a leader and had no care or understanding of how much damage he was doing to himself, his wife, and his effectiveness as a leader. He was completely blinded by his own lustful appetite.

Our interview even extended into creative explorations. I said, "Do you think being disciplined in certain areas (conversation & sex) of marriage foster growth in one's career?"

"Well, I think they make your marriage great. If you can have great conversation and great sex with each other I think you're going to be a much happier person, and general happiness can be increased. This has been supported by a lot of research. The happier you are, the more creative you are. I can get outside of myself and explore possibilities that are out there. "

In the end, for each person, whether male or female, rich or poor, infidelity will cause a great deal of pain in one's life. The most important human relationship in one's life can be held intact or destroyed on one agonizing decision. All those

participating in the exalted human bond we call
marriage can either grow themselves morally and
spiritually through their faithfulness to their partner.
Or, they can potentially ruin themselves through
base decision-making. For the leader, his or her
entire growth and ultimate success is built upon a
relationship that may not even concern his career on
many occasions. Faithfulness is a monumental task,
especially for those who are rising in rank according
to friends, social standards, their peers, the media
and monetary yardsticks. Nevertheless, it's up to
each person to remain faithful, joyous and effective,
or face the ridicule, distress and collapse of a fault
in one's character.

*My integrity is what it is today because of painfully
valuable lessons with consequences, born from
accountability to moral and ethical principles.*

—Col. Eric Kail

General Studies on Character

The lives of great leaders who have had their legacy destroyed or stained from their lack of personal discipline in the area of human sexuality reveal the errors of infidelity. The list of leaders who damaged their own leadership ability through a lack of discipline in the area of sexuality is long. The lack of self-discipline not only hurts a leader, but it also hurts their closest confidant. The pain can hurt to the core. No one is perfect, all humans have eyes and can be enticed by their natural desires in a flashing second, but indulging in unfaithfulness repeatedly is a task that eventually leads to a great fall in leadership or leadership potential.

Chapter #8

The Givers: Non-Profit

(Empathy and Compassion)

MISKEY

The road to Anne Miskey's office was a journey. That is the most sincere way I can put it. As the former CEO of the Downtown Women's Center, Anne Miskey led a team of over 100 staffers. She now serves as CEO of Union Station Homeless Services. She keeps herself occupied by working over 60 hours per week with many of the most disadvantaged individuals in the country.

The Downtown Women's Center is stationed in Los Angeles near the heart of Skid Row. Throughout the country, Skid Row is known for its high rate of homelessness. Currently, it has the highest homeless population in terms of population density within the borders of the United States.

I walked through Skid Row as I made my way to the Downtown Women's Center. For many, this well-known area is a frightening place. I saw trash throughout the streets and empty wine bottles on the ground. Trash bags and articles of loose clothing were stacked on the sidewalks of each block I passed. There were people lying on the sidewalks, and putrid smells of urine and feces. The smell was almost unbearable, but it definitely showed how forgotten this place had become.

Skid Row is only a few miles from the University of Southern California and the Staples Center arena where the Los Angeles Lakers play. In addition, it's just a couple blocks away from the elegant and impressive restaurants that flood the Los Angeles nightlife.

As I continued to walk, I wondered how these people must feel. Being homeless and living just a few blocks away from prosperity can be demoralizing. Was it their fault they were in this situation? Was it society's fault? These questions swirled around my mind until I was alarmed by the number of tents lined against the commercial buildings on each block. People were actually living in small tents! Worn shoes hung from poles, and music from 1990's styled radios filled the air.

Finally, I made it to the Women's Center. It was absolutely magnificent. I'd just walked through the worst sight I'd ever seen in my life (I'm not kidding; walk through Skid Row for yourself) and now I was in a multiple story building full of vibrant life and warmth. The Downtown Women's Center has a library, resting rooms for the women who reside there, balconies, a fabulous dining hall and the Mayor of Los Angeles was once served Thanksgiving Dinner there.

I was excited to see Anne Miskey, but slightly depressed and confused about what I previously saw. How could people live like that?

How could we allow others to live like that while we live in the richest country in the history of the world?

Instead of focusing solely on the negative aspects of my journey, I began to look forward to my interview. First, I stopped in the Women's Center Café. The women of the center created hand-made trinkets for sale to the public. These ornaments and charms were arranged throughout the café, and they were an incredible sight to see. The funds from the sales of the ornaments go back toward helping the center and women putting their lives back together. There were inspirational quotes on the walls, and the food served in the café was quite tasty. After spending a short time in the café, I made my way to the main building. I asked for the CEO. After a brief moment, I was kindly asked to take a seat. I waited for less than five minutes. In no time, Anne Miskey arrived.

She was extremely pleasant to walk with, talk with and be around. She was probably the kindest person I interviewed for my research on leaders. Mrs. Miskey has a big heart, truly cares about people and wants to make lasting change. That is why she moved to Los Angeles and worked in one of the most challenging areas regarding homelessness in the United States. Anne Miskey is not only a joy to be around and has a terrific sense of humor, but she stands as a highly educated woman. She is not all heart, she definitely has a mind. Mrs. Miskey left the corporate world to serve the public in the area of homelessness. Anne studied in Spain and France. She also spent time educating herself in Seattle and San Diego. She has a Bachelor's Degree from the University of Lethbridge and Master's of Divinity from the University of Toronto. Anne also made note of her preaching skills during our interview. Who knows, one day she may leave her job to preach full-time. Or maybe she already is preaching. She's preaching through her actions and not simply through her words.

For I was hungry, and you gave Me something to eat; I was thirsty, and you gave Me something to drink; I was a stranger and you invited Me in; naked, and you clothed Me; I was in prison, and you came to get Me.

—Matthew 25:35-36 (NASB)

While Anne Miskey spoke to me in her office, the leadership qualities of kindness and compassion became very prominent. She discussed humility, social justice and the idea of keeping her organization aligned with their basic mission. But kindness and compassion are the qualities that permeated through this woman's pores.

As we began our discussion, Mrs. Miskey talked about her decision to go into the non-profit world. She was unfulfilled in her role in the corporate arena and was really looking forward to making significant change around social issues and not simply doing charitable work.

After revealing these thoughts, I immediately countered her statements. I said, "What do you mean by charitable work?"

She said, "The kind of thing that helps a few people, but doesn't change anything for the majority of people. So, it's similar to the difference between feeding a person today and how we get to a point where we never have to do that again. In fact, we get them out of the system. We get them to rebuild their lives so that they don't need to go to a food bank."

I was alarmed by what she said. In the past, I'd helped individuals by contributing my free time to foodbanks. Our discussion was eye opening. She continued.

"I'm just using foodbanks as an example. We put all of our energy into putting food in a foodbank, and not putting energy into finding out why people are hungry and why can't they afford to buy their own food."

Mrs. Miskey's desire was to understand how to change the system and get to the larger issues regarding homelessness. Plainly, she wanted to see progress in moving people forward and not simply helping people with a cup of water or plate of food.

The idea of giving someone a meal or bottled water is definitely a kind gesture, but it doesn't contribute to lasting change. I believe compassion is one of the many driving forces that pushes Anne Miskey to make a contribution to those who sleep on the streets of Los Angeles. Many of us are too busy to leave our fabulous jobs in the corporate world to do something like this. Many of us are too tired to use our time off to focus on generating ideas and plans to help others in this destitute situation. Some of us think homelessness doesn't affect us, but it does. It affects tax dollars, government initiatives, healthcare costs and the very morale of a city. While the Downtown Women's Center focuses specifically on women enduring traumatic events in their lives, homelessness in general is a stain that we should all focus on removing.

Next, I asked, "What are you learning now? Especially with your staff, you have over seventy people on staff."

I was startled when she said, "We actually have over one hundred. I've learned that you can't forget the staff. We've forgotten the people who are there day in, day out, listening to people with health issues and aren't paid decent salaries. I think there is a quote from Richard Branson that says, I don't serve the client, I pay attention to my staff and they serve the client. If my staff has a wellness plan and get paid a decent salary, they will treat the client with respect."

A leader's team are the people who deal with the organization's issues daily on an intimate level. Anne Miskey sees her staff as those who do the difficult tasks because they are so committed to their organization's mission. Pay, wellness plans and respect are all things necessary leaders should give to members of their full-time staff. It seems like this should be an automatic gift given to team members, but these gifts aren't given to many employees.

The kindness of a leader permeates through the veins of an organization. Leaders who don't focus on their staff and solely worry about their own status, portfolios or press, eventually become those who lose what they've gained. When a leader focuses on their staff, they in turn forge themselves into a more cohesive and productive unit, which helps the organization meet its goals and function on a higher level. The focus a leader puts on her team actually brings the same energy right back to her because the productivity of the organization shines a light on the leader's leadership ability.

As our stimulating interview continued, I stated the following: "In your field, leaders seem to always be in a state of crisis. So how do you stop yourself from becoming desensitized to the issues you're trying to prevent?"

Mrs. Miskey replied by saying, "By knowing how to step away without hardening yourself. It's a real fine balance. I tell my staff, if you're a person who bleeds every time someone is hurt, you will burn out very quickly and you will not be able to make decisions that need to be made. I use the example of a surgeon. If a surgeon becomes overly involved in every patient he or she sees, he's not going to be effective. But if you cease to care about saving someone's life, then you shouldn't be doing the job either. It's a very fine balance."

With all the kindness and compassion necessary for working with homeless individuals there is a need for logic. The job done by the Downtown Women's Center is not simply a purge of feelings and emotions. There are goals, plans and intricate solutions being found to contribute to the work of ending and preventing homelessness.

Anne Miskey calls this compassion fatigue. When dealing with so much trauma, a team member or leader of an organization similar to Anne's can simply shut down. Ninety percent of the homeless women entering the center report being a victim of sexual violence. That is what has been reported. Anne believes the statistics are definitely higher. This doesn't even include many of the other issues that come with being homeless like the impact homelessness has on one's life expectancy or the likelihood of one's children being homeless.

As our discussion concluded, I was taken by the knowledge and understanding of the person sitting before me. I received years of experience and wisdom within an hour of time. As Anne and her team continue to do great work, others will continue to come alongside and create lasting change. If not, as a nation, we're in for a massive amount of trouble. With the ever-growing rate of homelessness in Los Angeles, the Downtown Women's Center is always open to receiving help from volunteers and support from those that generously give resources to help advance the mission of eradicating the ills of homelessness. To learn more about the Downtown Women's Center, go to www.downtownwomenscenter.org.

<u>WALTON</u>

Young Leader

(Age 35 and under)

The first leader interviewed for this book was Rebecca Walton. Rebecca is from Australia and the roots of her heritage are easily heard from her semi-thick Australian accent. She is sort of a bouncy individual, but quite direct and willing to get to the point of an assignment standing ahead of her. When she isn't biking, hiking or simply traveling through nature, she invests her time in helping others.

Mrs. Walton has seen the world. She's set foot in several continents, several countries and several cities. She has a girth of experience and world knowledge. Her experience, at such a young age, spans wider than many who have lived twice as many years as she has. Outside of her travels, bouncy personality and ability to venture into the unknown, Rebeca Walton resides in the United States.

Rebecca was stationed in Santa Monica, CA when we began our interview. We were quite acquainted with each other before speaking about the topic of leadership, and hearing her stories and trials were a voyage through the rough waters of the world.

Rebecca initially went to Africa at the age of nineteen. She found herself on this foreign continent during a break from her academic studies. It was a formative time in her life and career. She ventured into remote areas of Africa where the people seemed isolated and almost helpless. After her short trip to Africa, her desire to help grew. Exposure to isolation, pain and a human capacity for need may have stimulated this desire.

The general leadership principles of empathy and compassion are found once again in the life and work of Rebecca Walton. Like Anne Miskey, Rebecca has a great education and she's also spent time working in the corporate world. Her tenures included working as a finance analyst, business analyst and software project manager. Still, something draws her to the works she does for others, and it's likely driven by compassion and empathy.

Mrs. Walton is the Founder of Global Tribe-Africa. The non-profit organization Global Tribe has been active since 1992. Mrs. Walton has even served in the slums of Mexico while organizing her own missions as a high school and college student. She also lived in Zambia with the intent to improve her knowledge of mission training. In addition, Rebecca has built homes, schools, churches, and orphanages in several different countries.

As a leader, Rebecca Walton has improved the lives of many individuals. Her improvements have not simply tugged at her and the hearts of others, but they've contributed to significant change in the lives of others. While working in Africa, Rebecca and her team launched a group savings and loan program for women. At the time of our interview, she noted that, "We have a savings group with over one hundred and fifty women enrolled."

Many areas that Global Tribe frequents have areas with severe poverty. Under these conditions, adults of all kinds suffer, but women in particular face difficult challenges. As always, there are stereotypes and difficulties in attempting to gain access to loans or other sources of funding for women. In some cases, there are deeply imprinted cultural standards that have continued through history. And this is not simply in African countries; this is noticed throughout the world.

In the case of Global Tribe, organizing programs that allow women in need an avenue to learn basic or second-tier financial fundamentals is essential to success. When thinking about these financial learning programs a leader's empathy for others is extremely necessary. What makes Global Tribe venture out and do things like this?

Rebecca has paid a price for her work in Africa. I asked her, "What have you sacrificed in the past, and what do you currently sacrifice now to hold the leadership position you hold today?"

After very little thought, she answered, "I sacrificed my time and salary when I moved to Africa. I did not have a salary waiting for me, but a few people supported me during my trip. There were language barriers in Kenya, theft, corruption of all kinds, and I even contracted malaria during my stay."

I'll ask the question again, what makes a leader venture out and do something like this? Stepping out of your comfort zone to help others is one thing. But leaving your home and moving to another country is a huge decision to make. With this decision came the opportunity to live in a much better African community, but Mrs. Walton went to the area of those in need. She gave up her finances, her comforts, status and health to venture out and assist those that were miles away from her.

After meditating on Rebecca's words and the virtue behind her dramatic move, you can only conclude that though leaders like this aren't flawless, there is virtue permeating through their veins.

Having books or newspaper articles written about you don't give a person the empathy and compassion needed to make a major shift like this. Applause from the world doesn't help one make a life-changing decision like this either. The radical change that is required to learn a new language, new culture, stay far away from one's immediate family members or even try new foods is a bit jolting to the psychology of an individual. But if the fire burning in the leader is large enough to serve those intended, then with the right team, enthusiasm and knowledge, much good can be accomplished.

Rebecca's story reminds me of a well-known compassionate leader. She wasn't always well known. A small blue sweater helped ignite her passion to help people across the land of Africa. A woman who was once threatened, hungry and betrayed while trying to help those less fortunate than herself, now stands as a leader in overseeing operations that attempt to help those that are less fortunate progress in their lives. The organization also oversees the gathering and spending of massive amounts of dollars annually. This woman is none other than Jacqueline Novogratz.

After stepping away from the luxury and prestige of Wall Street, Jacqueline Novogratz went on to co-found Rwanda's first microfinance institution. After much toil, Jacqueline decided to move back to the United States. Next, she invested her time in education, learning at the Stanford Graduate School of Business. With this, she did not forget about her passion. In due time, she ventured back to countries outside of the United States to assist those facing the realities of poverty. While working in areas surrounded by poverty, Jacqueline faced illness, a lack of food, a lack of financial funding, corrupt individuals, corrupt groups, and power grabs from self-interested individuals. Through these trials, Mrs. Novogratz continued her mission, and with persistence, her mission to support others has in turn made way for her own advancement.

Acumen, the organization Mrs. Novogratz now leads, has since invested more than 100 million dollars around the globe to assist in the financial growth of individuals in search of economic prosperity.

Mrs. Novogratz started her mission to save the world at a young age. I believe she's come to learn like we all do that no one can accomplish that mission alone, but the empathy and compassion she's shown throughout her life for others has been astounding to hear and learn about.

The central idea of Acumen is to use monetary currencies as an avenue to stimulate entrepreneurial activities to assist in the uplifting of the poor. Would I say their efforts are working? I think so. Could their efforts be better? I think so, but the issue here is not simply the leader. Leaders don't do everything alone. It takes a group effort, and that is what Rebecca Walton and Jacquline Novogratz seem to understand.

It's not simply the leader; it's the team. To learn more about Global Tribe and support their work, visit www.globaltribe.com.

General Studies on Character

Misplaced empathy and compassion can lead to a sort of death. It can lead to something similar to an emotional freeze. Standing as a sort of messiah for an individual or group of people leads to tremendous burnout. We can only do so much as leaders, but each of us can make an effort to do our part in assisting with progress. With all of the empathy and compassion necessary for leadership, this does not mean leaders walk around without a backbone, or that great leaders are afraid to take a stand against a worker or a fellow leader who is behaving inappropriately. Remaining empathetic to others needs is important, but too much empathy can be disastrous.

Chapter #9

Mustard Seed Faith: Religion

(Fulfilment)

CANALES

Picture yourself rounding third base in a Los Angeles Dodger Blue Uniform. The crowd erupts as you approach home plate, sweating, panting and shouting with excitement. Your family cheering along in the stands and the roars of the crowd rise with the passing of each second. That was a portion of life for Pastor Joshua Canales. A portion of life he lived before the call.

As a high school student, Pastor Canales was drafted by the Oakland Athletics, but chose to continue his education at the University of Florida and the University of California, Los Angeles. Finally, in the year 2001, Pastor Canales received his childhood dream. He was drafted by the Los Angeles Dodgers. With this eventful past, Pastor Canales now serves as the Lead Pastor of Mission Ebeneazer Family Church in Carson, California. Although his life is far from normal, Pastor Canales lives and speaks like a humble man. Every morning, he gathers himself as he rises from his bed and thanks the Lord for another day. We can all gather nuggets of wisdom from this act. This simple act is fulfilling in itself. The realization that every day is precious, that life is a gift and everyday we're given breathe is a day of joy and prosperity, no matter what conflicts occur in our lives.

After gaining a greater understating of Pastor Canales' time playing for the Dodgers, I wondered what brought about his change of heart. Who would cast aside a Major League Baseball Contract for separate pursuits? Pastor Canales was in the prime of his career when he decided to leave baseball. Not only was this decision risky, but it was also courageous. The vast majority of Americans would not turn down millions of dollars to go serve their community as a local pastor. Pastor Canales left the cameras, fans, riches and pride that come along with being one of the best athletes in the world. Competing in athletics professionally is a common dream for young males, and Pastor Canales simply tossed that monumental dream away. My first thought was what would make a person do this? What did his family think? What about his wife? They were set financially for the rest of their lives. But, Pastor Canales made a courageous decision. It was about doing what he knew he should be doing with his life, not chasing a childhood dream.

In my attempt to gain a greater understanding of his dilemma I asked my question. "Why did you quit playing for the Los Angeles Dodgers? That's a once in a lifetime opportunity."

He said, "I guess it boils down to calling and purpose. When you reached out, you emailed me because you had a purpose. When the Lord called me, he had a purpose for the call. He had a greater purpose and I had to get prepared for full-time service."

My next inquiry included the following: "I think that was a radical move. I applaud you for it, but I want to play devil's advocate. Someone could say, why did you have to leave baseball? You could have prepared in the offseason or on your off days. Why did you have to totally leave baseball?"

Pastor Canales noted, "There is no half way, either you're all in or you're not. So, for me, if I was going to be dedicated to baseball and my career, that's what I was going to do. But, if God called me to preparation and going to seminary after finishing my degree at UCLA, then I was going to go all in and train and prepare for pastoring."

The sacred calling that leads pastors all over the world to quit jobs, risk their homes and empty their lives for others is frightening. It can be downright painful in many cases. What if the radical change in career doesn't work? Where will they receive funds to take care of their families? What if they end up homeless? Will they go back crawling to their jobs, or will they remain on their sacred journeys? This doesn't even include the gut-wrenching negative comments members of the clergy receive from friends, family or spouses who think they've made the wrong decision. Though I don't believe Pastor Canales received an extraordinary amount of negative feedback regarding his decision to leave professional sports, there are people who do.

Sacrifice isn't sacrifice if you don't have options.

—T.D. Jakes

I directed yet another question toward Pastor Canales. "What have you sacrificed in the past, and what do you sacrifice today to hold the leadership position you hold today?"

After releasing a deep grunt, he paused, then said, "As the oldest of three boys, I've always felt that I was the one to step up in the time of need. I've sacrificed my playing career, and even my education."

It took Pastor Canales eight years to complete his Master's Program. His seminary education at Fuller Seminary was put on hold once he stepped in as the Lead Pastor of his home church. Due to his father's illness, Pastor Canales put his studies on hold and contributed his efforts to his home church completely. He suggested that his younger brothers continue their education and career pursuits. It was a moment of leadership, a moment where leaders rise to find solutions to massive and unforeseeable issues.

Pastor Canales fulfillment seems to come from giving. Giving himself. Giving himself to the congregation he serves. Giving himself to his community in Carson. Giving himself sacrificially to his family in a time of unusual pressure and giving his heart, mind and soul to God. Again, leaving the enjoyable life of a professional athlete was a sacrifice. But fulfillment for Pastor Canales seems to come from following God's plan for his life and not submitting solely to the pursuit or wishes of the general population.

Clarity came to Pastor Canales early in his playing career. During his collegian years, Joshua Canales ventured out of California and headed for the east coast. There he competed against many skilled athletes with a close friend.

During practice, Joshua Canales stepped up to bat. The next swing would bring about a monumental change in his life. Waiting for an incoming pitch, Canales swung, and hit a line drive. Coincidentally, his college friend was not paying attention. His back was facing home plate and his attention was not on the quickly approaching ball. To everyone's dismay, the baseball leaving Canales' bat hit his friend in the head.

What happened next led to a time of grief, sadness and deep contemplation. Joshua Canales' friend was sent to the emergency room. Being unconscious, the young man eventually passed away.

This painful moment is something most human beings can't imagine. A friend's life was gone in a matter of minutes. How does your self-esteem change? How do your parents comfort you? What about your friend's parents? How does one comfort their grief?

In his own words, he said, "That was a crucial event. Not a turning point, but a formative moment in my life that really helped crystalize my character, who I am. Really having to look in the mirror and say, who are you? What am I about? What is life about? Is it about baseball? Is it about people? That was a point in my life where I had to persevere at twenty-one. Baseball is just a tool, an avenue, a gift. It's not a means to an end. It made me grow up a lot. The Lord preserved me during that crisis when I lost one of my dearest friends at the hands of my own self. I know it was an accident. If it wasn't for people that were supporting and praying for me, it would have been a difficult thing to get through. I came out of it seemingly unscathed, but fortified and more sure of who I am and of my faith."

Most will not have to endure many of the things that Pastor Canales did, but tragic events do have the potential to shape our lives for the future. Coming to an understanding of what life really encompasses, finding a mission, gratitude, and a foundation for living is a complete course in the art of fulfillment. It's not simply padding investment accounts, sitting on influential boards or wielding great power. Fulfillment is personal for each individual, and it is typically found away from the limelight. Crowds don't contribute to the joy of a fulfilled individual. It is not the crowd. It is the mission, the service and in Pastor Canales' case, following God's plan for his life.

BLACK

As a child, Chaplain Barry Black quickly approached the start of a long spiritual journey. The journey started with his mother developing him into a student of scripture. Chaplain Black received a nickel from his mother each time he memorized a verse from the Bible during his adolescent years. The wisdom developed from the memorization techniques would soon be worth more than the nickels he received.

Currently, Dr. Black holds the position as Chaplain of the United States Senate. Senator Bill Frist appointed him to his post in 2003, and he is the first African American to hold the position. With roots in the Navy, Dr. Black served over twenty-seven years in the United States Navy as a chaplain. He earned two Ph.D.'s and has a highly impressive library volume of over 10,000 books.

Chaplain Black has a history of connecting individuals through prayer. His national prayers have caused shifts throughout our nation. Dr. Black's work in Washington, D.C. doesn't stop there. At least once a week, Capitol Staff meet for prayer and Bible study. As one would guess, Chaplain Black serves as a major contributor during these meetings.

While leading over 7,000 people in his role as chaplain, Dr. Black found time in his schedule for this interview. After taking time to deliberate over a number of potential questions, I asked Chaplain Black the following: "What is your greatest achievement as a leader thus far?"

Dr. Black answered, "That I married my wife Brenda and that God has blessed us with three wonderful sons. Being a parent can be quite a challenge and finding the right woman [is important]. I've been married to her for forty-four years and that's an amazing achievement."

I learned a valuable lesson while working in Congress. I would rise from my bed around 5am, read, study, eat, exercise and get ready for yet another beautiful day. I was working in what many believe is the center of modern civilization, but I couldn't seem to completely enjoy my time there. Some think that working in the Longworth or Rayburn Buildings are the pinnacles of success in the political arena, but something was missing.

I would later come to find that it was a lack of complete fulfillment. Yes, the lunches were great, and the offices were majestic. But fancy offices and wonderful food won't calm a rattled soul. It's certainly obvious why Chaplain Black leads thousands of individuals in his current position. He's come to understand that the foundation for fulfillment is not in his title, luxurious office, large platforms to speak on, attention received by news cameras, or financial gain. The foundation for complete fulfilment begins with pleasing the Creator and engaging with those you love.

Subsequently, I asked, "What skills did you gain from your time in the Navy, and how did they transfer over to leadership in the political arena?"

Chaplain Black answered swiftly, "I learned how to mobilize people towards a shared objective. When you come to a place as a leader, you seek to listen first. You don't come in with a bag of tricks. You listen, then you're able to mobilize people toward a shared objective because they own the objective."

This type of leadership is not natural. It goes against human nature. Putting others before ourselves sounds nice to say publicly, but how many of us do this on a consistent basis? There are times when we may have had intentions to put others first, yet we fail to follow through with our good deed. We typically fail to follow through because we get too busy, we don't have patience, or a more urgent matter arises. Chaplain Black explained what all great leaders come to know after spending valuable time leading groups. A leader who fails to recognize the goals of the group soon finds himself alone.

Great leaders receive fulfilment in their work when they help advance others through life. This also includes the opportunity to view their group growing individually and in a team environment. Ask any spectacular parent, uncle or aunt. Fulfilment comes through seeing their young grow and achieve. Those that force their young into pursuing their own desires end up causing their children and themselves misery.

Great leaders leave ripples. The ripples are the individuals who grow and pass along the quality goads of truth to the next generation of leaders.

I pressed Chaplain Black further regarding the topic of fulfillment. I asked, "Periodically, you hold the minds of those who make, research and study the laws that govern our nation in your hands. What messages are you trying to use to influence their decision making?"

Dr. Black answered with the following, "One of the important messages I try to share with them is found in Ecclesiastes 12, 13 and 14. After writing the book of Ecclesiastes, the writer said, let us hear the conclusion of the whole matter, fear God and keep His commandments. For this is the conclusion of the whole matter. For God shall bring every work into judgment with every secret thing, whether it be good or whether it be evil. So, I remind them of their accountability. That they are accountable to God and that He is the only

constituent that you absolutely must please. And
that one day, what is done in the dark will be
brought to light."

*As I grow older I pay less attention to what men
say. I just watch what they do.*

—*Andrew Carnegie*

Darkness is a fertilizer for evil. It is quite
natural for evil to rise in high places. But wise
leaders don't attach themselves to it. Defending
ourselves against evil may lead us to leave a job,
start a new business, vote against a highly supported
measure, remove an employee, or even relocate to a
new city. Others may oppose our decisions, but if
we continue en route with the desire of our Creator,
then we will eventually reach fulfillment. Decisions
like these on many occasions are painful. The loss
of income, status, or relationships create unwanted
experiences. Our opponents can become our close
family members, friends or even disgruntled
mentors.

In all fairness, a blow from an opponent
doesn't always wound leaders, but a blow from a
partner or close family member can sting and leave
emotional pains for years to come. In these
instances, we look to our Creator. We look to our
state of joy, we look to our state of peace, and
finally, we look in our bathroom mirrors. Hopefully,
we are able to stare ourselves in the face and

become overjoyed with the decisions we've made as leaders.

Skillful leaders find fulfillment in helping others grow. Following the plan for our lives and basic focus on our work is an essential part of fulfillment. In hopes of gaining a greater understanding of this concept, I asked, "I think the book of Proverbs is your favorite book. It is also mine. Is there a reason why you quote the book so much?"

Chaplain Black revealed the following. "I think Proverbs is the greatest success manual ever written. And I quote it a lot because of all of the books of the Bible, it probably had the most transformative impact on my life. Proverbs 24 says, the hand of the diligent shall rule. I was blown away by that. You mean all I have to do is work hard, be diligent, and I will have positions of leadership? Proverbs 12:29: show me a person diligent in his or her business, he or she will stand before kings and queens and not ordinary people. Wow, that's an amazing promise. Proverbs 6:6-10: go to the ant, you lazy bone. Consider its ways and be wise, who having no overseer, stores in the summer in preparation for the winter. That tells me, be a self-starter. Don't wait for someone to crack the whip."

In my opinion, laziness is a spiritual crime. Some may even call it an offense toward God. At its root, it can be looked upon as a treasonous act against one's self, their family, and their community. One who fails to act is a person who never reaches his or her potential. The same goes for someone who seems to have reached the heights of success. If we stop advancing, we begin to degenerate.

As we neared the conclusion of our interview, we spoke about four more areas of fulfillment. I asked, "Do you have daily rituals that have served you in building your moral character?"

He said, "You need to focus each day on four areas. The Bible says of Jesus in Luke 2:52, and Jesus increased in wisdom, so that's intellectual increase. Stature, that's physical fitness and health. In favor with God, that's spiritual. And humanity, that's social. So, I am interested in my intellectual development, physical, spiritual and my social development. I spend at least an hour each day praying the scriptures in personal devotion. That is my foundation for development in these four areas."

I asked, "When it comes to leadership, have you gotten rid of all of your character flaws?"

"I really don't think that anyone gets rid of all character flaws. Even to the end of life, there will be things you are working on. Trying to be like Christ is the mark we're pressing toward, but we will be pressing toward it until the day we die."

Everyone makes mistakes, so being a person of integrity does not mean you haven't committed a moral or ethical violation, ever. It means having the strength of character to learn from those 'misbehaviors' and seek continual self-improvement.

—Col. Eric Kail

CHAND

Dr. Chand is not the typical spiritual counselor or business leader. One of his favorite sayings is, "The only way to grow your pain threshold is more pain. You will only grow to the threshold of your pain." The quote is true, but hard to swallow. Most people, at least most sane people, do not rush for the thrill of pain. But Dr. Chand's words can help anyone who wants to grow personally and advance as a leader.

Dr. Chand was born in India. He moved to the United States during his formative years and met his wife while attending Seminary. He has served as a pastor, president of a university and now speaks to leaders around the world. These leaders include pastors, politicians and business owners. During his travels, he still finds time to preach the Gospel and write great books. Two of his books, *Leadership Pain* and *Who's Holding Your Ladder?* are outstanding works on leadership.

I first met Dr. Sam Chand in Long Beach, California. He was giving a lecture on leadership at a church. He probably remembers going to the church, but I'm almost certain that he doesn't remember our public conversation. During his talk, one of the topics he discussed included building trust and the power trust brings in an organization. After he concluded his remarks, he opened the meeting for questions. There was a period of silence in the room, and I wondered if I should raise my hand to ask a question. Luckily, someone else did, so I had more time to deliberate. After Dr. Chand answered the question, a second hand went up. He answered that question just as easily. Then, the room fell silent again. The organizer for the night said, "Well, since we have no other questions."

With that comment, my hand shot up. The organizer walked toward my seat and handed me the microphone. I thanked Dr. Chand for speaking with us, then asked, "A few minutes ago, you said everything revolves around trust. My question to you is, how do you increase trust quicker?"

Dr. Chand took a moment and paced back and forth with his head down. In that instance, I thought I stumped him. I wasn't happy about it, because that meant I wouldn't receive the answer to my question. But it did feel good thinking I asked a pretty good question. Finally, he looked up and said, "Crisis."

The entire audience roared with laughter. He didn't give another answer, but he asked me a question instead. He said, "What do you do?"

I replied by saying, "I just left my job." After that statement, he fell silent again. You could see the wheels turning in his mind. Dr. Chand went on to explain how Angela Merkel, then the Chancellor of Germany, became Time Person of the

Year. He continued by showing that her efforts to solidify a country in crisis caused those living in the country to trust her and follow her at an even greater level. With those courageous acts, her leadership influence became greater.

Dr. Chand's message concerning trust and crisis was excellent for that time in my life. At that time, I was in a crisis. Less than a month before that meeting, I left a job working for an elected official. I thought that some of the things I was being asked to do went against my personal beliefs and the route I had envisioned for myself to become a person of integrity. So, I left that job and entered a Master's program at a local seminary. Leaving a secure job in my early twenties was no easy task. You worry, wonder, and attempt to calm yourself knowing that standing for the ethical principles you believe in have to pay off someday, even if there is a sense of sacrifice at the present moment.

As leaders that were previously interviewed like Dr. Tabaee suggested, you quickly find that when you leave a job like the one I had, you lose your steady paycheck, you lose your 401k, your medical benefits, you lose your political status, political power, and relationships that are attached to being affiliated with the nature of that work.

The entire ordeal was a crisis in my life. What would I do next? How would I pay the bills? Is doing what one believes the right thing to do really worth it? At the time, I believed it was, and I still believe it now.

Almost three years later, Dr. Chand and I spoke again. This time, Dr. Chand was in Atlanta, and I was in Los Angeles. As always, he was sharp and insightful.

I asked, "What is one attribute leaders need to lead in an excellent fashion?"

He said, "You have to be totally invested in the other person. If you're not totally invested in the other person, you can still lead them, but not to the degree you could."

Dr. Chand answered two questions here, and one of the questions wasn't asked. He gave illuminating thoughts on potential and fulfillment. Dr. Chand's thoughts on potential are no different than the ordeal a college quarterback endures while being drafted to the professional ranks. Owners, general managers, and head coaches crave leaders that will fit into their organizational structure.

Typically, the leader of an NFL football team is the quarterback. Thus, a coach is not only looking for someone that is intelligent and has great athletic ability. They are looking for someone who has the potential to excel in the role as the leader of the team. This encompasses much more than athletic ability. It includes many of the qualities previously examined in this book: ethics, morality, humility and a persistent will to win.

To be an excellent leader, one has to fulfill their potential or come extremely close to fulfilling it. Leaders can't do this by keeping their eyes on themselves. Selfishness only dwindles one's leadership ability. Your leadership is dependent on how well your followers do. If you're doing well as a leader, but all of those you lead are miserable and drained emotionally, you're more like a tyrant. Highly respected coaches in athletic sports are those who not only win, but they eventually mentor assistant coaches who are prepared to become successful head coaches. These assistants are targeted and promoted to the position as head coach for different organizations and move on to become respected leaders in their own right. But their potential to learn and grow began when they were assistants, learning from a leader who was totally interested in their growth.

Regardless of your position, industry, or where you might fall on an org chart, if you want to become a world class leader, you must realize that the only way you can reach your potential is to first help your team achieve theirs.

—Brian Souza

In the same instance, Dr. Chand answered the question on fulfillment. In order to lead in an excellent fashion, leaders need to be fulfilled. This typically means they are happy, excited to be alive and venture into the day's tasks. This means they enjoy what they do and are most likely healthy physically, mentally, and emotionally. Once again, fulfillment comes when we take our eyes off of ourselves and give careful attention to the development of those we lead. It is not fulfilling to rise as a leader when the rest of your team remains stagnant. In these situations, the leader knows his or her actions are not promoting peak performance through their organization. Stagnation is actually more like a tumor. Those that want to grow eventually leave, and those that stay who have the potential for growth begin to shrink and never reach their potential.

An unfulfilled leader is one on a never-ending chase to find a spiritual high that will never be found by looking solely at oneself.

I questioned Dr. Chand again, "Why does character in leadership matter? There seems to be so many leaders that get by without it."

He said, "At the end of the day, it matters who's going to gauge your leadership. If you think that your stockholder, stakeholders, or church members are going to gauge your leadership and call it successful, then you'll live a certain way. But when you realize that at your funeral, the only people that will realize if you were successful is your family, then you will work on your character.

So, when you die and I die, it matters little what others say about you. It matters what your family says about you. . . Psalms chapter one, it says blessed is the man who walk not, next it says stand not, next it says sit not. Walk, stand, sitting. That's the anatomy of sin. You keep walking you're fine; you stand, you are opening yourself to harm. When you sit down, it's too late."

After pausing to take in the wisdom he gave me, I asked, "What is your greatest achievement as a leader thus far?"

"I think it's still ahead of me. I've had achievements in social life, academia, church life, as a consultant. God has been good to me. You know, one achievement peaks another one, then it peaks the next one. You know, I think my greatest achievement would be being married to the same lady for thirty-nine years, having two amazing children, an amazing son-in-law. My greatest achievement would not be corporate, it would be my family."

There are many times when I'm working that I think about my sister or my nieces. I think about my best friends or my cousins, the Dixons and the Heads family. Hopefully, many of us do this. I check on them when I can, but as always, I can improve. Infrequently, I think about my funeral. As Dr. Chand suggested, the people who really matter are my family. There are times when I contemplate who will be there. Who will sit in those seats, watching as my body lies lifelessly? My co-workers? Maybe some, but most likely, not many of the co-workers from my past jobs will be there. The people who will be there will be my family. It's a wise thought to hold as we live our lives.

One of the more impressive things I learned about Dr. Chand was how much he invests time with his wife. As noted earlier, Dr. Chand has a hectic travel schedule. He speaks and consults with leaders and audiences all over the world. During our interview, he slipped in a nugget of wisdom. He revealed that while on the road, he speaks to his wife twenty times a day or more.

After my disbelief fizzled, I was amazed. I asked him again just to be sure I didn't misunderstand him and to reassure myself. He persisted, "They're never long. Sometimes it's just a text. Like, how are you? It's nothing long."

As our interview concluded, I asked Dr. Chand a final question. I thought he would be out of wisdom to give. I was absolutely wrong. I asked, "Is there anything you would like to add on the topic of character in leadership?"

He concluded his remarks with prudence. It went straight to the heart. After a long pause, he mentioned the following: "You know, character is a pretty slippery subject. Because how we judge ourselves and how we judge others are quite different. We judge others by their deeds and we judge ourselves by our intentions. The Bible tells us that our heart is deceitful. It says who knows the heart. That is where self-judging of character can be deceitful. That's why character depends on perspective. There are people who may say, I have great character and you may watch their lives and say, no, not at all. Character is one of those subjects in which judging yourself is really not the wisest thing. But character still is the most important thing. The best way I can describe character is that it's a slippery subject."

When pride comes, then comes dishonor, but with the humble is wisdom.

—Proverbs 11:2 (NASB)

****

<u>*General Studies on Character*</u>

For what does it profit a man to gain the whole world, and forfeit his soul?

—*Mark 8:36 (NASB)*

The places of worship in the modern world are wonderful places to gather with others and take a path towards improving individually and collectively as enlightened beings. With all of the positive aspects of Sunday morning gatherings and midweek activities on church campuses throughout America, there are still areas of improvement for those leading and attending church services.

Some see these flaws and leave to discover themselves and their God with other techniques. Some stay and become accustomed to the madness they've discovered before their eyes. Neither of these options are the best routes to take. Refraining from all church activities for those who want to grow spiritually is not a wise road to take. Try attending another church. And knowingly cooperating with leaders lacking character is a foolish decision. Either demand a change or leave.

Members of the clergy have a special position in leadership. They deal with the most important aspect of the human being. The aspect of the human being I'm describing is the human soul. While no spiritual teacher living today has attained the ideal of living a perfect life throughout their time on earth, they still have the ability to assist in the fundamental establishment of spiritual growth for many individuals.

While the failures of religious leaders are numerous, redemption is available. Redemption is available, but it is up to those who have made the mistake of dismantling their own character and conscience to begin the practice of improving their personal character.

Former church leaders come to mind when I recall character failures that have caused damage to thousands of trusting church goers. Some church leaders have faced scandal and jail for embezzlement. The financial theft is disastrous for communities of faith and those looking for a peaceful community.

The well-known words written thousands of years ago still ring true today. You reap what you sow. This message goes to leaders and those emerging as leaders. One can be blessed with great intellectual abilities, attractive looks, the ability to connect with others emotionally, and even an overwhelming amount of financial backing. But, without established character and the personal intention to improve one's character, the end goal of leadership is disastrous. Join the fight for character. It will affect your bloodline.

<u>**Leadership Tools:**</u>

<u>**Traits Great Leaders Have In Common**</u>

1. Many leaders stumble up on their vocation.
    (Judge Cullers, Mrs. Walton, Dr. Chand)
2. The first people to shape a leader's character
    are their parents.
3. Compassion, empathy, and integrity are the
    top traits leaders spoke about regarding
    qualities leaders should possess.
    (Sec. Panetta, Mrs. Miskey, Dr. Matthew)
4. The leaders interviewed consistently spoke
    about not being passive when one sees
    unjust treatment or immoral behavior.
5. Leaders trade time with their families and
    the enjoyment of personal luxuries for their
    goals. But they refrain from trading time in a
    way that hurts their families.
    (Mr. Farfsing, Dr. Chand, Pastor Canales)
6. Refrain from trading your morality for
    advancement in your career.
    (Sec. Panetta, Judge Cullers, Mrs. Fine)
7. Great leaders enjoy challenges and set high
    goals.
    (Mrs. Miskey, Mr. Farfsing, Sec. Panetta)
8. Celebrated leaders take their job or
    leadership position to help and serve the
    public.
    *(President Castro, Mrs. Walton, Dr.
    Tabaee)*

9. Leaders don't panic in a crisis; they think their way out of it.
(Judge Cullers, Sec. Panetta, Mr. Grimshaw)

10. Many of the leaders interviewed found mentors through constant and close observation.

11. When dealing with failure, leaders champion the quality of persistence. They always continue to move forward and bounce back to reach their goals in a more ferocious fashion.
(Mrs. Fine, Judge Cullers, Mrs. Walton)

12. Leaders try to make other people on the team look good.
(Mr. Berkus, Dr. Tabaee, Dr. Chand)

13. Leaders seek to connect. They bring people with various goals from different environments together for the greater good.
(Mr. Berkus, Dr. Harley, Dr. Black)

14. Prayer is a daily practice that builds moral character.
(Pastor Canales, Dr. Black, Dr. Chand)

15. A large portion of the leaders interviewed for this book believe their greatest achievement is still ahead of them.
(Mrs. Miskey, Dr. Chand, President Castro)

16. Leaders "light up" when they talk about reading.

17. Leaders have the ability to see multiple sides of an issue and either blend them together or

make the most reasonable choice in a time of conflict.

18. Every leader interviewed worked towards attaining a quality education.
19. The vast majority of the leaders interviewed are married.
20. The vast majority of the leaders interviewed believe in God or a higher power.

<u>Dave Berkus:</u> Dave Berkus is of Jewish descent and completed a term of service in the United States Army. He is an angel investor and has experience as a TEDx speaker. As an angel investor, Mr. Berkus has a rate of return of 97% per year. Just four of his accounts amount to about 90% of his returns. His investments include over 140 technology ventures, and over 161 investments in total. After starting a business at age fifteen, Mr. Berkus went on to control and hold the position of chairman in multiple companies. Additional business honors include producing 16% of automated hotels worldwide and becoming a leader for an Inc 500 company. As a philanthropist, Mr. Berkus has given grants to non-profit organizations and scholarships for students pursuing higher education. His general philosophy on business can be found in the books he's written.

Q: Why did you desire to become a business owner and investor?

A: My family has been my model going back to my grandfather, and I remember none of my family members had ever worked for somebody else. They all created businesses and worked for themselves. It was expected. When I created my

first business at the age of fifteen, it was a
phonograph record business. I worked out of my
bedroom. Then later on, I created tapes for
schools, colleges (USC, UCLA, Stanford) and
churches. It turned into a full-time business and
I ran that business for nineteen years. . . I sold
the company, then began investing in other
entrepreneurs, primarily because those two
businesses I built, I didn't have coaches. I
wanted to be able to give money to entrepreneurs
that needed it. At the same time, give them other
things beyond money itself.

Q: What added value have you given to others as
you've made investments?

A: My work has led to me making investments in
176 companies and another 130 investments in
the companies that did well. And in other cases,
letting the company die when the company
wasn't getting any traction. Twenty-seven of the
companies have been sold or gone public,
twenty-eight of them have gone broke and the
rest are moving wherever they are. I've been
teaching the entrepreneur about the use of
corporate time, providing relationships for their
business, analyzing the process of a business or
getting their product to the market faster, and
finally setting the context. Are they too early or
too late for the market?

Q: What have you sacrificed in the past and what do you currently sacrifice to hold the leadership position you hold today?

A: In the past, I hope I wasn't sacrificing family time. In the past, I kept asking my kids if I wasn't shortchanging them because I would begin programming at five in the evening and I wouldn't stop until 2:30am. I would come home by three and get up at seven to see the kids off to school. But sometimes I was never there in the evening and that worried me a lot. I became a scout master so I would always be there for weekends and Monday night meetings. Now my kids are grown. They said they didn't miss me at all because I was always there when they thought they needed me. I flew an average of 5,000 miles a week during that second business. I would leave on a red-eye Monday night and be back on Friday.

Q: You are a wealthy man; how do you combat pride in your life?

A: The last fifteen to twenty years is that I've focused on non-profits as much as I have coached other people. My own success has been a result of other people's success. In the non-profit world, I've donated a third or more of all of the money I've ever made, including to a college I used to attend. And boy scouting.

Q: How do you deal with pain and what do you do to relieve the pressure of leadership?

A: I love to work with technology with my hands, and I will often build things, whether that is software or hardware. I build things where I overcome challenges. That's a physical as well as a mental exercise. During the summertime, I swim every day.

Q: How did you choose your mentors, and what characteristics did you see in your mentors that you wanted to see in yourself?

A: I didn't have any coaches in my first business. When I got through the first level of growth in the computer company, the second company–we grew from two million, to four, to eight, to twelve, to twenty, to thirty million–I found myself wanting to associate with others who I looked up to. . . So, I wanted to associate with some of the CEO's of the hardware and software companies in Orange County. They were people I looked up to. They were larger than I was and had grown faster. So, I joined a group called Southern California Technology Executives Network. I joined it in 1987.

Q: What is one attribute leaders need to lead others in an excellent fashion?

A: Subordinating their own ego. To understand that your success is based upon the people that

you hire, and second, that you train, and third, that you let loose when necessary. Servant leadership allows you to grow by selection and training of others that are as good or better than you are.

Q: There seems to be a fine line between greed and wanting to do well for your family. Is greed the major factor that leads to the decline of a business leader?

A: With greed, you're going to burn the relationships that could have made your life much better. You have to look at much more than greed.

Q: Has the Amazon ordeal been one of the greatest mistakes you've made in enlarging your leadership capacity?

A: I'd say the Amazon story is so much fun to tell. I was giving a talk to the Angel Capitol Association and when I came off the stage, someone I'd known tapped me on the shoulder from one of the Angel Associations who said, you know Dave, you keep talking about how your one hundred thousand dollars would have been thirty-three million during the IPO, when the price of Amazon was $1.97. Let me show you where it would have been if you would have held it through right now. At the time, the stock was at $1,000. The hundred thousand would have been well over eighteen billion dollars. I titled the talk Smiling at Success, Laughing at Failure, because you have to laugh when you find these things you could have done that you passed up for various reasons. At that time, I didn't want to fly my plane a thousand miles to get to a company and help a young CEO Jeff Bezos. I would have learned more than I would have taught, but a thousand miles seemed too far away. I've learned to be humble.

Q: Who have been your biggest critics, and how have you handled them while maintaining your character?

A: I've been sued five times, and once as a CEO. A CEO once claimed that I forced him to get a bank loan, but as his chairman I did nothing of that kind. I wasn't even aware he went out to get a loan. We are now friends again. I was sued after another company dissolved. Another time, I was sued by the cousin of an entrepreneur. The cousin invested in the company, and it failed and I had been the chairman and I invested too. The cousin sued me saying I had induced him into investing. You're getting a theme there. I had nothing to do with the cousin investing into his own cousin's business. I won them all. It underscores the fact that there is some risk coaching these entrepreneurs because of the passion of these entrepreneurs that sometimes leads in a strange direction.

<u>Dr. Barry Black:</u> Dr. Black's extensive background includes almost thirty years as a chaplain in the United States Navy. He rose to the rank of Rear Admiral and Chief of Captains. After being appointed to his current position in 2003 by Bill Frist (R-Tennessee), Dr. Black became the first African American in the history of America to hold the position of U.S. Senate Chaplain. In addition to pastoring the thousands of individuals who work in the U.S. Senate, Dr. Black is a known Christian of the Seventh Day Adventist denomination. Finally, Dr. Black holds a Ph.D. and has a personal library volume of over 10,000 books.

Q: Why did you desire to become a chaplain or a pastor?

A: My mother was baptized when she was pregnant with me and she asked for the Holy Spirit to place a special blessing on her unborn child. After I was born, I was told that I seemed to have a precocious interest in spiritual things. I enjoyed church, little teaching opportunities and I never wanted to be anything other than a

minister. I think that is because God honored my mother's prayer.

Q: Who helped form your character most?

A: I was exposed to the great books of the western world in the 1960's, which was a set of books, at least sixty-four volumes by Britannica, and they have all of the great philosophers. Epictetus, William James, Sigmund Freud, David Hume, Montaigne, Aristotle and Plato. And I just started reading these writers and their great books. Like Augustine's Confessions, Thomas Aquinas' Summa Theologiae, Aristotle's Rhetoric, Aristotle's Nicomachean Ethic.

Q: What has been your greatest achievement as a leader thus far?

A: That I married my wife Brenda, and God has blessed us with three wonderful sons. I've been married to her for forty-four years.

Q: What are you learning now?

A: I am focusing on becoming better at praying. I think prayer is something that we don't do enough of, and yet it is the one thing that the Bible tells us to do continuously. 1 Thessalonians 5:17 says pray without ceasing. No other thing does God tells us to do without ceasing except pray. I am learning that there are many types of prayers. There is lip prayer (reciting phrases), head prayer (prayer while reading the

scripture), and the third kind of prayer is heart prayer (it becomes a mantra in your life).

Q: What skills did you gain from your time in the Navy, and how did they transfer over to leadership in the political arena?

A: I learned how to mobilize people towards a shared objective. When you come to a place as a leader, you seek to listen first. You don't come in with a bag of tricks. You listen, then you're able to mobilize people toward a shared objective because they own the objective. I've also learned to be sensitive to the diversity in religious traditions. As a Navy Chaplain, I had to be concerned about meeting the needs of Jewish people, Hindus, Islamic people, making sure they have an Imam. So, it broadened my outreach. It taught me how to respect all people and be inclusive of all people.

Q: Periodically, you hold the minds of those who make, research and study the laws that govern our nation in your hands. What messages are you trying to use to influence your decision making?

A: One of the important messages I try to share with them is found in Ecclesiastes 12, 13 and 14. After writing the book of Ecclesiastes, the writer said, let us hear the conclusion of the whole matter, fear God and keep His commandments. For this is the conclusion of the whole matter. For God shall bring every work into judgment

with every secret thing, whether it be good or whether it be evil. So, I remind them of their accountability. That they are accountable to God and that He is the only constituent that you absolutely must please. And that one day, what is done in the dark will be brought to light.

Q: I think the book of Proverbs is your favorite book. It is also mine. Is there a reason why you quote the book so much?

A: I think Proverbs is the greatest success manual ever written. And I quote it a lot because of all of the books of the Bible, it probably had the most transformative impact on my life. Proverbs 24 says, the hand of the diligent shall rule. I was blown away by that. You mean all I have to do is work hard, be diligent, and I will have positions of leadership? Proverbs 12:29: show me a person diligent in his or her business, he or she will stand before kings and queens and not ordinary people. Wow, that's an amazing promise. Proverbs 6:6-10: go to the ant, you lazy bone. Consider its ways and be wise, who having no overseer, stores in the summer in preparation for the winter. That tells me, be a self-starter. Don't wait for someone to crack the whip.

Q: Did you once say your mother used to pay you for memorizing scripture?

A: A nickel a verse.

Q: Do you have daily rituals that have served you in building your moral character?

A: You need to focus each day on four areas. The Bible says of Jesus in Luke 2:52, and Jesus increased in wisdom, so that's intellectual increase. Stature, that's physical fitness and health. In favor with God, that's spiritual. And humanity, that's social. So, I am interested in my intellectual development, physical, spiritual and my social development. I spend at least an hour each day praying the scriptures in personal devotion. That is my foundation for development in these four areas. For my intellectual well-being, I'm always reading a difficult book and an easy book. For my social development, I go out of my comfort zone and reach out to people. I introduce myself on planes and I incorporate these things into my day. But most important, obviously, is that one hour of devotional reading and praying the scriptures.

Q: How did you choose your mentors?

A: I choose my mentors through the great books. For instance, if I want to understand scientific thinking and haven't read Descartes, then there is an awful lot of information that I'm not even aware of. Then great people in history, Winston Churchill, Franklin Roosevelt, John F. Kennedy, Gandhi, Martin Luther King Jr., they certainly

blazed trails that were exemplary. They inspired me to follow in that train.

Q: What are the greatest mistakes you've made in enlarging your leadership capacity?

A: I think being afraid of failure. So being reluctant to try something because I think it's too difficult. I learned that failure is actually a stepping stone to eventual success. When I was completing a second doctorate, a Ph.D. in Psychology, I had to take one final class in order to finish my dissertation and I flunked the mid-term for that class in three consecutive attempts. Meaning I flunked, dropped the class and took it another semester. Flunked again, dropped the class and took it another semester etc. And I still managed to get a B+ in the class the third time. So, I had to learn not to be disillusioned by failure, or what appeared to be failure–to keep pressing toward that mark, as Paul said.

Joshua Canales: Pastor Canales is the Lead Pastor of the Rock Church in Carson, California. The Rock Church is a growing church with over 3,000 members. As a coveted baseball prospect, the Oakland Athletics drafted him out of high school. He was subsequently drafted by the Dodgers in

2001 after excelling on the field at UCLA. Pastor Canales played professional baseball for three years, then pursued his call into sacred service. He attended Fuller Theological Seminary and attained a Master's Degree.

Q: Why did you quit playing for the Los Angeles Dodgers? That's a once in a lifetime opportunity.

A: I guess it boils down to calling and purpose. When you reached out, you emailed me because you had a purpose. When the Lord called me, he had a purpose for the call. He had a greater purpose and I had to get prepared for full-time service.

Q: I think that was a radical move. I applaud you for it, but I want to play devil's advocate. Someone could say, why did you have to leave baseball? You could have prepared in the offseason or on your off days. Why did you have to totally leave baseball?

A: There is no halfway; either you're all in or you're not. So, for me, if I was going to be dedicated to baseball and my career, that's what I was going to do. But, if God called me to preparation and going to seminary after finishing my degree at UCLA, then I was going to go all in and train and prepare for pastoring.

Q: What is one word or phrase that would describe the mental attitude you try to maintain during a crisis?

A: Persevere. I've gone through a lot personally. Whether it's my education–it took eight years to finish my Master's degree because I was a father, pastor and community member.

Q: How did the incident in your college years affect your character?

A: That was a crucial event. Not a turning point, but a formative moment in my life that really helped crystalize my character, who I am. Really having to look in the mirror and say, who are you? What am I about? What is life about? Is it about baseball? Is it about people? That was a point in my life where I had to persevere at 21. Baseball is just a tool, an avenue, a gift. It's not a means to an end. It made me grow up a lot. The Lord preserved me during that crisis when I lost one of my dearest friends at the hands of my own self. I know it was an accident. If it wasn't for people that were supporting and praying for me, it would have been a difficult thing to get through. I came out of it seemingly unscathed, but fortified and more sure of who I am and of my faith.

Q: What is one attribute leaders need to lead in an excellent fashion?

A: Keep your word. Work harder than anybody else. And number three, what you do, do it quickly.

Q: Is there a major flaw you typically find in leaders who have a big scandal or fail to reach their potential?

A: People fail for all different types of reasons. Whether it's greed, power or position. I think it's when people are not happy with themselves and are not content. They pursue things they think will make them happy. So, I think the answer would be insecurity. They aren't really secure with who they are or what they do. They try to fill their lives with empty substitutes. I think it comes back to insecurity.

Dr. Joseph Castro: Currently Dr. Castro serves as the President of California State University, Fresno. During his more than twenty-year career in education, Castro has served in leadership positions within the University of California system at the Berkeley, Davis, Merced and Santa Barbara campuses. Standing as the first in his family to go to college, Dr. Castro earned a Bachelor's Degree in Political Science. In addition, he earned a Master's Degree in Public Policy from the University of

California, Berkeley and a Doctorate in Higher Education Policy and Leadership from Stanford University. Castro is a 1984 graduate of Hanford High School, where he was the editor of the newspaper and played varsity tennis. In addition to his leadership roles, he's taught Leadership and Health Policy at the University of California, San Francisco.

Q: What was the purpose behind your desire to become a university president?

A: I think it started with my recognition in college as a student that my life was being transformed by my university experience. I was a first-generation college student, and son of a single mother. I was the first in my family to experience the university education. As I was experiencing that, it dawned on me how important universities are in our society. They are one of those institutions that make a huge difference in people's lives and alter the trajectory of their lives. So, I became curious about universities and I began to study them.

Q: Other than yourself, who helped form your character most?

A: It would be my grandparents. But of the two, probably my grandfather. I didn't have a father. He was the most significant male in my life and it

was really his character that shaped my own. I observed him as he dealt with different people. He started out as a farm worker, but by the time I came around, he delivered beer. He was just so good at working with people, I would go in his truck and watch him and I'd help him to. He always had this ability to connect with people. I never saw him lose his temper, even though I'm sure he was upset from time to time. He was very good at staying calm and cool.

Q: What has been your greatest achievement as a leader thus far?

A: I have a bias. The work I've done here at Fresno State has been the most impactful work I've done in my career–the fact that I grew up here, and this area that I serve as president is an area that historically has been underserved, historically has had higher poverty rates, higher unemployment rates, and it is a very diverse population. This university is making a huge difference in lives by graduating more students than ever before. I also helped found UC Merced earlier in my career.

Q: What pitfalls have you tried to avoid?

A: I like to use the word temptation. What I've found is that there can be a temptation to choose an easy path. Because of the nature of the work I do now, there are people who have strong opinions, whether it's a wealthy donor or a legislator or an influential faulty member who might want to try and apply pressure to me to do something that they want me to do. If the leader is not strong, over time they could succumb to those temptations, and I think that's where the character comes in and the integrity. When I have to make a highly contested decision, I go back to what the mission of the organization is. The mission is to boldly educate and empower students for success. And what are our values as an institution? This is my home base when I have to make a decision. The other pitfall is to realize that it's not about me. It's about the people we serve.

Q: You wrote an article for the Fresno Bee last year. The first quality you put down regarding good leadership in the Bee was listening. What are you seeking to extract from the students and your staff when you engage with them?

A: Listening and learning are probably the two most important things that I do. It enables me to hear different perspectives. I try to lean in and listen to the different viewpoints and especially when somebody is saying something completely different than what I'm thinking. Because that is the opportunity to learn. What happens with some leaders over time is that they think they've figured it out, and they get into learning traps.

Q: You lead thousands of students each year. What sort of foundation are you trying to lay in their minds for their future?

A: I believe that they're a part of our next generation of leaders. I think the students here know that the focus is on making sure that they're successful and I want them to be very honest with me and all of my colleagues about their experience. They will send me feedback through email, social media and while I'm walking on campus. I appreciate that. Now, that doesn't mean that I will fix their problem. It means that I am aware of the problem and I can get it into the right hands and have the decision made.

Q: I found it extremely difficult to find university presidents of four-year institutions that were of minority descent. Of course, you have historically black universities, but it was very difficult outside of that to find minority presidents. So, you having this position shows that you are special. What do you think separates you in terms of leadership from the rest of the pack?

A: There are national efforts to change that and I am mentoring people who want to change that. We need to have more people preparing for these positions. How do I answer this? I am the first person of color, I am the first person born in this region, first person born in California to be

president of this university. The other seven all came from outside of California and they were all fine people. The edge I have is that my credentials are at least as good if not better, but the most important thing is that I understand the culture of this region and the people that we serve. It was very natural for me to come here and focus attention and energy on the students. I didn't know the culture of this university, but I know the people here. I lived here, my wife is from here, I've had relatives come here. So, from that perspective, it's like putting a suit on that fits just right.

<u>Dr. Sam Chand:</u> After traveling from India to North America as a young man, Dr. Chand continued his education until he earned a Ph.D. Dr. Chand travels around the world speaking and consulting with business leaders, politicians and leaders in various nations. He is a former University President and he has served in the role of Senior Pastor in a Christian church. Currently, Dr. Chand serves as CEO of the Sam Chand Institute where he's written many books on leadership, hosts conferences, provides advice for sacred and secular groups, and also engages in business consulting.

Q: Who helped form your character most?

A: I would say my parents. You know, character is not taught, it is caught. I was blessed to be in a pastor's home who actually walked what they taught.

Q: What pitfalls have you tried to avoid?

A: I have avoided relationships that would take me down a slippery slope. I've also avoided temptations that come during difficult times to bail out.

Q: How do you combat pride in your life?

A: Having a good family will do that. You can be on somebody's platform, but at home you're just dad, grandpa, a husband. Nobody takes you seriously at home. No one holds you on a pedestal. After you live life a little bit, you realize you're not all that. Pride begets arrogance, then you become dishonorable of people, then it comes back to bite you. I don't think there's anybody who would say to you, I have fought my battle with pride and I don't have any challenges anymore. I think that is the insidious nature of humanity.

Q: What is your greatest achievement as a leader thus far?

A: I think it's still ahead of me. I've had achievements in social life, academia, church life,

as a consultant. God has been good to me. You know, one achievement peaks another one, then it peaks the next one. You know, I think my greatest achievement would be being married to the same lady for thirty-nine years, having two amazing children, an amazing son-in-law. My greatest achievement would not be corporate; it would be my family.

Q: What are your strengths?

A: I want to grow. I want to be a perpetual learner and I have a deep sense of curiosity.

Q: What have you sacrificed in the past, and what do you currently sacrifice now to hold the leadership position you hold today?

A: In the past, my family. I sacrificed a lot of quality time with my family. I mean that in a bad way. That was definitely not a good thing for me to do. In the truest sense of sacrifice, where it hurts, I'm not sacrificing anything right now.

Q: As a leader, have you gotten rid of all your character flaws?

A: You may have a nanosecond of that, but the only time you will be like that is when you're with the Lord. I have not experienced that yet, and I don't think I will.

Q: How do you deal with pain and relieve the pressure of leadership?

A: I usually talk to somebody, because pain has a way of growing and becoming dysfunctional. You start swimming in your own negative juices and feeling sorry for yourself. I talk with my wife and my friends. They may not always have the answers though.

Q: Do you have any daily habits that help build your moral character?

A: I pray, talk to my wife and talk to my kids every day. I'm on the road a lot, so I talk to my wife 20-30 times a day. But they're never long.

Q: What is one attribute leaders need to lead others in an effective fashion?

A: You have to be totally interested in the other person.

Q: What were the greatest mistakes you've made that have grown to enlarging your leadership capacity?

A: My greatest mistakes were people mistakes. People I should have dealt with earlier on, but for whatever reason, I did not. I talked people into staying when it was really time for them to leave. A lot of times, I have allowed people to hold me hostage. In the way of how that decision would hurt me, and I was escaping my pain. Not realizing to go up, I had to deal with my pain. My biggest challenges came from not dealing with people issues.

Q: Is there a major flaw you typically find in leaders who have a scandal or fail to reach their potential?

A: Yeah. I think before the big earthquake hits, there were fault lines that they did not recognize and people around them did not recognize. Or others rewarded them for their behavior. Let me give you a biblical example of this. Psalm Chapter One. It says, blessed is the man who walk not, next it says stand not, next it says sit not. Walking, standing, sitting. That's the anatomy of sin. If you keep on walking you're fine. If you stand, now you are exposing yourself to harm. And if you sit down, it's too late. So, fault lines are forming in people's lives and we need to be aware of that.

Q: Is there anything else you would like to add on character in leadership?

A: Character is a slippery subject. How we judge others and how we judge ourselves is very different. We judge others by their deeds and ourselves by our intentions. The Bible tells us the heart is deceitful. It says who knows the heart, and that's where self-judging of character can be deceitful. Character is one of those subjects in which judging yourself is not the wisest thing, but character is the most important thing. That's why I describe character as a slippery subject.

Judge Mark Cullers: While playing tennis at the University of California, Los Angeles, Judge Cullers received a Bachelor's Degree. He continued his education and received a J.D. from George Washington University thereafter. Prior to his term as a judge, he served as a federal prosecutor in Fresno, California for twenty-seven years. During his tenure as a prosecutor, he served as Chief of the United States Attorney's Office in Fresno. He's tried dozens of federal jury trials to verdict, and also teaches criminal trial practice at the San Joaquin College of Law. Currently, he holds the position of Judge on the California Superior Court of Fresno.

Q: Why did you become an attorney?

A: Originally, I wanted to go into international law. My major was Political Science and I wanted to go into foreign service. I decided to take the traditional law firm route and that got me into a law firm back in Sacramento... I did an administrative law hearing and a very good friend of mine was very praiseworthy of the way I handled the hearing. I found that I enjoyed cross-examination. She encouraged me to apply at the US Attorney's Office. There was an opening in the Fresno Office and I took the position.

Q: Other than yourself, who helped form your character most?

A: It would probably be my father. He's passed on, but he was a very intelligent, principled and opinionated man. He was worldly. He used to take my brother and I to the symphony. The other person would be a family friend named Nat Pitt. He was my tennis coach.

Q: It took you two or three times to pass the bar. What made you stick it out?

A: It took me four times. What made me stick it out was the belief of some people around me, my parent's beliefs, and also my own beliefs. I knew once I passed, I could be a good attorney. So, I said, this is just a bump that I need to get over. That's not to say I didn't have my doubts by the third or fourth time. I knew that if I just worked hard enough, I would make it through.

Q: What is one word or phrase that describes your mental attitude during a difficult situation in trial?"

A: Don't panic. Just roll with it. When you panic, adrenaline pumps through your system and you can't think straight. You get scared. If you can't think straight, you can't think your way out of a problem.

Q: What are your strengths?

A: That's probably for other people to answer. I don't give up easily and I don't get discouraged easily. I believe in myself.

Q: What are you learning now?

A: I don't know everything, and there is a lot to learn: learning to communicate with people, treating them with respect. I don't want litigants to feel intimidated by the court. I want them to feel like they can receive a fair hearing.

Q: What are you reading?

A: I read every night. I go through phases. I go through my Civil War phase, my WWII phase, my biography phase. Believe it or not, I'm in my WWII spy phase. I'm reading MI6 & MI5 British spies who were active in WWII. Very fascinating reading about how they were double agents with the Germans.

Q: What have you sacrificed in the past and what do you currently sacrifice now to hold the leadership position you hold today?

A: I think what you sacrifice most is time. Being the Chief of the Office, you spend time in the office on the weekend. Now as a Judge, I just wish I had more time because there is just so much to learn.

Q: As an attorney, how did you deal with pain?

A: I played tennis and I read. I haven't won one hundred percent of the cases I've tried, but that's ok. I think you learn more by losing a case than by getting a conviction. When you get a

conviction, you think you're the greatest
prosecutor in the world, but that's not
necessarily true. When you lose, it causes you to
say how can I be better? How can I present a
better case? What didn't the Jury understand?
Its good in life to lose every once in a while
because it causes you to have self-reflection.
When you keep winning all the time, you never
stop to pause.

Q: How did you choose your mentors?

A: By observation. I choose the people I
admired. There were Judges and attorneys, even
defense attorneys I admired. Mostly people I
observed and said they have a trait I would like
to have.

Q: Why do you think character in leadership
matters? There are so many leaders who get by
without it.

A: I don't think a good leader is one without
character. I think it would cause those who
follow that person to go down the wrong path.
Leadership with character uplifts people, makes
people better, uplifts society. Character is how
you act when nobody is looking. You can't turn
on and off character. Character has to be
ingrained in who you are. Character is a 24/7
thing. Truthful, honest and ethical. It also
includes empathy.

Q: Is there a major flaw you typically find in leaders who have a scandal or fail to reach their potential?

A: Ego. Lawyers have a term called robitis. Attorneys put on the robe and then they have robitis. All of a sudden they have this sense of power and omniscience. They think they can treat people disrespectfully or bark at people. You have to stay humble.

Q: How do you do that?

A: Reading! You read about others, their lives, their struggles. It keeps me humble. Having a sense of gratefulness keeps you humble. A sense of God or the divine, however one wants to cast it. I learned this from my mother. I'd come home after a tennis tournament with a trophy after winning the tournament and she would tell me to go scrub the floors. It kept me real.

Ken Farfsing: Mr. Farfsing began his celebrated career after completing an undergraduate degree in History at the University of California, Berkeley. He's worked for a number of cities in California. This includes forty years of involvement in local government and twenty years of service as a City Manager for the cities of Carson, Signal Hill and South Pasadena. In addition to his time as a City

Manager, Ken Farfsing is a water policy expert.
Finally, he is working on his first book, which
covers the history of the City of Signal Hill.

Q: You were in retirement. Why would you come
out of retirement and take this position?

**A: Challenge was a part of it. I really believe that
cities need to be effectively managed. We all live
in cities, and we all want them to survive and
thrive. And you have to have good city
management to do that. I've always been a
people person. I like people. Public service was
ingrained in us as we grew up as kids. My
brother was very active in politics. The first
candidates I recall as a kid were John Kennedy
and Richard Nixon. My brother got involved in
Robert Kennedy's campaign. I remember that
whole period of turmoil. Obviously, Martin
Luther King was assassinated, you had the riots
in the 60's and the Vietnam War. So, growing up
in that era, I recognized that government was
really critical in our lives and you had to have a
government that was accountable to its citizens.
You need an effective government to help people
move forward. In our house, we always had
political debates. My mom was fairly liberal and
my dad was pretty conservative. At dinner, there
were seven kids, so around the dinner table we'd
have debates about the Vietnam War. My dad**

felt we should go to the army. My mom felt we should go to Canada (laughs from me). It was pretty wild. My mom liked Cesar Chavez; we didn't eat lettuce.

Q: What is your greatest achievement as a leader thus far?

A: I think my greatest achievement in Signal Hill was to move them out of the Great Recession, and we didn't do any employee layoffs. When I watched the city budget drop, I was really concerned about it. We had no idea how deep the recession would be or how long it was going to last. I was there for nineteen years and we only had two unbalanced years. Basically, stabilizing the place financially and getting it back on its feet financially was a major accomplishment.

Q: What are your strengths?

A: My experience. I have thirty-nine years of experience working in cities. Coming in here, I've had to rely on all thirty-nine years. I also like to network and I like to learn from other people. I think building a network of the best and the brightest is great for getting you through sticky situations. I'm not afraid to try new things and make mistakes. You tend to learn more from your mistakes than your wins. And I like to give credit to others. When you look at the council, they have to put their ego on the line and they have to put up their own finances on the line when they run. Money in politics can be corrosive at times, but it's a necessary evil. You have to have money now to run for office even for city council. You need about 100,000 to run for office in a city like Carson. So even if an idea starts with me, I like to bounce around an idea and I like them to take credit for it. Myself and the staff did all the work, that's what we're here for, but they should get the credit. I have trouble talking about what are your strengths. I like people to feel like we're giving good public service.

Q: What are you reading?

A: I'm reading a book about the greatest migration in U.S. History. It's about the black migration out of the South. It's a fascinating book. I really wanted to understand how all of that came about. What was it like to be black in the Jim Crow South? What obstacles did they encounter and how did they migrate? I'm a history major. It helped me put into context some of the struggles people have had.

Q: What pitfalls have you tried to avoid?

A: We have a code of ethics. So, if the Mayor comes to you and says you can't tell everybody else. This is what I want you to do, but I don't want the council to know. You have to sit the Mayor down and say, 'Look, I have to treat all council members equally.' That's one I run into

all the time. Some councilmembers don't like
other councilmembers. It's like high school
sometimes.

Q: What have you sacrificed in the past and what do
you sacrifice now for the leadership position you
hold today?

A: I think you realize you're finite as you get
older. Time is a gift God has given you. You
don't have a lot of time as a City Manager. You
don't have as much time as you would like to
spend with your family. You can't travel. I think
in the nineteen years I spent in Signal Hill, I took
a more-than-one-week vacation only twice. In
the last twenty-five years, I only took a two-week
vacation twice. It's hard on your family and its
hard on your wife. You almost have to quit your
job to do those things. On my bucket list, I've
always wanted to go to Turkey to see all the
Roman ruins, but you can't do that in a week.
The problem is the way the cities are staffed
nowadays. You don't have backup. There are no
number twos. When you come back, you have
stacks of work on your desk. So, when I go on
vacation, I call it a work-vacation. I take projects
with me and answer emails half of the day.

Q: Do you have any daily rituals that have served in
building your character?

A: I get up on time (laughs). I'm an early riser.
And I'm a planner. Each day I try to advance a

project that I'm working on. When I was in
Laverne, there was a 100-acre cow pasture. I did
a plan, it was a five-year labor of love. We
brought in an economist and he said it would
take at least twenty years for the business park
to fill up. It's interesting; I was in Laverne in
1985, and when you go back now, it's a nice
business park. So, the economist was right, but
maybe another person would have given up on
this. I didn't have staff, so when I had spare time
I'd work on it. It showed me if you set an
objective and you keep working on it, eventually
you'll get there. Stick to it.

Q: What are the greatest mistakes you've made in
enlarging your leadership capacity?

A: You make so many mistakes. It would have to
be personnel or budgeting. When I was in South
Pasadena, we had a utility tax and we were
unsure if it would pass. And the council had a
contingency plan that if it didn't pass, we would
have to lay off people in every department, so I
had to go talk with each employee that was going
to be laid-off. I felt that I should go talk with
them personally instead of just sending a memo
out. Because I felt it was important. How would I
want to be treated if I was going to be laid off?
Luckily, the tax went through. This has
happened in every city I've been in. Right now,
in Carson, we have a tax measure in November,
and if it doesn't pass we're going to have to do

layoffs. People come to me and say Ken, what's going to happen to me if the tax doesn't pass? I think back to the experience, about how horrible the experience was for people who may have their whole life change.

Q: Why do you think character in leadership matters? There seems to be so many leaders who get by without it.

A: I mean, look at Weinstein. If you go back to Stephen Covey's book, really the measure of a person is what people think about them when their life ends. He has an analogy: you're at your own funeral and you have the ability to hover over the congregation and hear your epitaph. I've always believed that basically what you have in life is your good name and your character, and if you compromise that, you've lost it all. The fame doesn't matter, the money doesn't matter. That's all kind of peripheral stuff. Character really does matter at the end of your life. It does come into play as you move from city to city. People hear of your reputation or know you, and it gets to a point where they trust you.

Q: Tesoro has one of the largest gasoline production facilities on the west coast, and it's in Carson. The city received about 45 million from that deal. How do you negotiate a deal like that without falling prey to Tesoro? You have to look out for so many different interests–the city's interest, your interest, the people's interest, the business' interest.

A: It will be the largest facility west of the Mississippi. Well, I guess the way I look at it, there has been a structural deficit in Carson for a long time. I think they're proud of the services they provide for the community. But the council is very reluctant to raise taxes on the residents. There are affluent families here, but there are also working families and some people living in poverty. So, there is a moral part of the equation. Then you have a very large business, you had refineries here before the city was incorporated in 1911, but when you think about it, you have over 100 years of refining in this community and the damage it's done to the environment. It was before the Clean Air and Clean Water Act. You have the residents who deserve certain amenities and very good people that work for Tesoro, but historically, they have a heavy footprint on the community. So, we called it a community benefits agreement. The money that came from Tesoro would go towards benefiting the community. I didn't really have any second giving's about negotiating things.

<u>Lauren Fine:</u> (YOUNG LEADER)

Hearing the story of a 14-year-old boy helped turn Lauren Fine into a social entrepreneur. She is dedicated to making sure children have a voice within the criminal justice system. Charged with murder, the 14-year-old boy was tried as an adult in a Pennsylvania court. He was subsequently convicted and sentenced to life without parole. At the time, this was a mandatory sentence in Pennsylvania for a juvenile convicted of a homicide. It appalled Fine, who was then working with children in foster care, homeless shelters, and in court as a Zubrow Fellow at Philadelphia's Juvenile Law Center.

Lauren Fine currently serves as co-founder of the Youth Sentencing & Reentry Project in Philadelphia. Her academic career includes a Degree in History from Yale and a J.D. from Duke University. Previously, Mrs. Fine clerked for Judge Strawbridge of the US District Court for the Eastern District of Pennsylvania. She's also worked with children in foster care and homeless shelters. Lauren Fine is a TEDx speaker and occasionally jumps on trampolines to relieve stress.

Q: What is your greatest achievement as a leader thus far?

A: Following our ideals and our vision, which was ambitious and audacious and a little bit crazy, and creating something in reality that reflects our vision. We haven't had to compromise the values that we have.

Q: I'm aware of the time you spent volunteering in prisons during your law school years. Why have you decided to take this venture on full-time? You could work for a big firm, make a lot of money and do this work part-time.

A: It's funny because that's a question that's been asked by my family many times. As you know, the work is not lucrative. So, that creates its own challenges. This is more than a full-time job to me. We wish there were more people alongside of us, and we wish we weren't working eighty hours or more a week. It feels like no matter what we do, we need more time and resources to do what we do, and do it right. And it's not something that I felt should be a part-time gig. It's bigger than a side project. I felt called to do this.

Q: What pitfalls have you tried to avoid?

A: When you lose your morality in service of anything, you're lost. A subset of that is how to speak your mind so you feel that you're not being silenced, but that you're also effective. Sometimes, I feel that there is a tension between those two things because there are things we see

and that we in some ways feel complicit in. Working in a system that is so deeply flawed, racist and oppressive, I wish I could get up and scream and stomp my feet and really just call attention to it. Then there is the tension between our larger goals and what we want to accomplish. We feel that we have to pick our battles and we have to be strategic in the way that we voice concerns and shine light on issues. That is a pitfall I've fallen into. There are pitfalls that include not caring about the way I say things and I think about how it has an impact on people's lives.

Q: I read the book *The Ethics of Capital Punishment*, and it noted your state. The book suggested that it has one of the highest rates of minorities on death row. So, do you think the problem is education or household income?

A: I think it's yes and… I think those things are a part of it. We have a school system here in Philadelphia that is being underfunded regularly and I think that is certainly a piece of it. We are investing more in prisons and in retribution than we are in educating children. I think that has disastrous consequences, and we see that in our work all the way up to the death penalty. As a side note, there are definitely people doing great things to try and address that. But I think its deeper than education. I think the criminal justice system has always been, or at least for very many years, has been a mechanism for state control and to perpetrate racism. And I think the death penalty is a perfect example of that. It's sentencing children to life without parole. So, it's sentencing children to die in prison. You may have come across that we did execute children until 2005 in this country. That's when the Supreme Court said that we could no longer impose the death penalty on children under the age of eighteen. To give you some hard facts really quickly, here in Philadelphia where I work and live, 89% of kids charged as adults, which is the area I focus on the most, are kids of color. That to me is a staggering statistic. Around the country, you're ten times as likely to be sentenced with life without parole and to die in prison if you're a child of color than if you're a white child.

Q: Are there ever moments in your work where you feel scared, nervous or in a state where you don't know what you're doing? And how do you handle it?

A: There are times like that every day. We created this organization from an idea in our heads. There were a lot of unknowns and there were many things we had to learn on the job. We always talk about the fact that we're building the plane and we're flying it, which is an inherently challenging and uncomfortable place to be because we are constantly confronting

challenging situations in terms of the substantive—but also, how do you create an organization that's sustainable, ethical and viable?

Q: Why do you think character in leadership matters? There seem to be so many leaders who get by without it.

A: Well, I guess that depends on how you define character. Because anyone who's a leader getting by has character, but it might just be a different type. I never want to walk into a room and have to feel embarrassed to tell anyone what I do professionally or about any of the choices that I make. Being true to your principles and your perception of morality often leads to success in other forms because you're able to make better choices and inspire others to come alongside and share your vision in a way that cutting corners doesn't allow you to do in the long run.

Q: Is there anything else you would like to add on character in leadership?

A: We really try to take a partnership approach. I'm a lawyer and I don't talk about "my client." I don't describe people in those terms. I look at it more as partnership. That we are very honored to partner with the people we work with and whose lives we are let into on a daily basis. It's a privilege that people let us into their lives during very difficult situations. We can otherize people

**and create barriers. We can label people with
artificial division. For us, it is really important to
acknowledge that our work can only be as
effective as the folks that choose to allow us into
their lives.**

Michael Grimshaw: In addition to receiving a
degree from California State University, Northridge
and taking graduate courses at USC, Mr. Grimshaw
is a veteran in the business arena. His experience
includes working with dozens of companies like
IBM and CISCO. Dr. Grimshaw has worked in
various business roles, which also includes
consulting and angel investing. In his role as
professor, Mr. Grimshaw teaches entrepreneurship
and a number of other courses at California State
University, Dominguez Hills and Marymount
University. Finally, Mr. Grimshaw's experience
includes time in the military and a legacy of starting
companies in Silicon Valley.

Q: You started your businesses early, and you
founded quite a few companies. Would you tell new
entrepreneurs to skip college and do the same thing?

A: I would never tell new entrepreneurs to do that. 95% of business owners have college degrees.

Q: Why did you become a teacher and why are you interested in entrepreneurship?

A: Because that's where you make the money and it's the most fun. Average income for an entrepreneur in the United States is $170,000. Those are small business owners, those are people who have been in business for many years. Now, I would not say Amazon and Google are entrepreneurial companies anymore. They aren't start-up companies anymore. They were at one point. I think on average, about 15% of the population are entrepreneurs.

Q: Why is it so hard to be an entrepreneur?

A: Because you are your own worst enemy. Fear, uncertainty and doubt in your mind will keep you from doing anything that is out of the ordinary. It's like any skill. If you practice it, you will become good at it. And you will never go back. You will never go have a job somewhere.

Q: When you're in the start-up phase for your company, are you going off of instincts? Of course, you're looking at your numbers, but are you making decisions off of instincts a lot of the time?

A: Yes. But they're calculated instincts. You weigh all the facts and look at everything, but in

the end, it's a gut feel. It's based on experience, intuition, a lot of things.

Q: Other than yourself, who helped form your character most?

A: Personally, I never knew my dad. I never met him. And my mom was married a number of times. She died at fifty. So, I never really had a man in my life, someone to guide me or coach me to what manhood was like. The closest was a stepfather I had. He was a famous actor, a character actor. I probably felt the closest to him. I got in trouble with the law early on and he helped me. He was not a great role model; he was an alcoholic, smoked like crazy and had a number of wives. But he took me in as his son right away, and I found that he listened to me and understood me most. And my mom, she was my guiding light.

Q: What are the greatest mistakes that have grown to help you in enlarging your leadership capacity?

A: I would say some of the decisions I made about employees. Making decisions that I wasn't comfortable making. Usually when we're parting ways. That's painful. Making a decision that will affect someone personally.

Q: Why do you think character in leadership matters?

A: Because we don't have any (laughs).

<u>Dr. Willard Harley</u>: Dr. Harley is an entrepreneur. He received his Ph.D. in Psychology and Degree in Artificial Intelligence at the University of California, Santa Barbara. As a psychologist, Dr. Harley had thirty-four clinics across the State of Minnesota. In addition to restoring marriages, Dr. Harley owns a non-profit called Marriage Builders, he hosts a radio program and has written numerous books which have sold millions of copies. Dr. Harley has been married for over 50 years.

Q: Why did you become a psychologist?

A: It's a long story, but my father was a psychologist, but I grew up believing it was witchcraft. I studied physics and I was interested in science. I was working on artificial intelligence when I was contacted by someone in the Psychology Department at the University of California, Santa Barbara. And they said they were looking for someone with a computer background. At the time, I hadn't taken a single course in psychology. They said I could get into their Ph.D. program without a Master's Degree, and I got my Ph.D. three years later. As I mentioned before, people kept coming to me with

their marital problems, so I did an internship in marriage counseling. We talked previously about that internship. The director of the program got divorced and they were talking about 90% success rate in saving or improving marriages, and I knew from the inside that they were not successful at all.

Q: Were you doing free counseling?

A: Not at that time. What I found was romantic love was missing in most marriages. I never came across a single couple, ever, who got divorced when they were both in love. So, my argument was that if I can teach you how to be in love with each other, you'll never get divorced. So, the secret to saving marriages is to prove to a couple that they can be in love with each other again. So almost all of my writings are about creating love in marriage.

Q: Someone may say, why have you given so much time to helping marriages?

A: Basically, God has a plan for our lives. And if you're interested in God's plan, you'll see the markers on the road. People are coming to you with their problems. You better know how to solve them.

Q: What has been your greatest achievement thus far as a leader?

A: The books I've written. And I run Marriage Builders, the website, and I'm able to help hundreds of people. The basic concepts that I write about are things that have been read by millions of people. *His Needs, Her Needs* has sold over 4.5 million copies, so in that sense I'm a leader. But I'm not really a born leader. I don't really like leading.

Q: Really? Why not?

A: To me, wisdom is a work in progress. And I wouldn't be a good cult leader because I don't believe everything I say is true. I don't know what's false, but I don't know for sure that anything's true. So as soon as you tell people that, they lose confidence in you (laughs). So, my feeling has always been that a good leader is inspirational and a good leader is motivational. I also have a beautiful wife and a great marriage.

Q: What are your strengths?

A: I'm very intelligent. God gave me a good mind. I have a high IQ. My greatest strength is that I value intelligence in everybody. I believe that intelligence is what makes us human.

Q: What are you reading?

A: I read Science America. I've read it since I was in college. I read books on archeology and geology. And I love astronomy.

Q: What pitfalls have you tried to avoid?

**A: My goal in life aside from serving the Lord is
to not hurt anybody. I used to have a terrible
temper, terrible anger problems. I overcame it.
So, my great pitfall would be hurting someone,
but I haven't. I would be terribly upset with
myself if I intentionally hurt someone.**

Q: How does a good marriage support a leader and
a marriage filled with tension or distress damage a
leader?

**A: I have a wonderful marriage, and my wife is
just a saint. And I would say that my life
couldn't have possibly been as successful without
her. We've been married for 54 years and we're
both in love with each other. Without her, I
think a lot of the things I've done wouldn't have
been as fulfilling. I think your fulfilment in life
comes by sharing your life with someone. So, I'm
a big advocate of marriage.**

Q: Do you think being disciplined in certain areas
(conversation & sex) of marriage foster growth in
one's career?

**A: Well, I think they make your marriage great.
If you can have great conversation and great sex
with each other, I think you're going to be a
much happier person, and general happiness can
be increased. This has been supported by a lot of
research. The happier you are, the more creative**

you are. I can get outside of myself and explore possibilities that are out there.

Q: You've studied human nature for a while now. Do you ever think a leader's character becomes fixed out of habit?

A: I think almost everything we do is from habit. The creativity that exists in people is much smaller than they think, so your leadership style will be habitual no matter how hard you try to not make it that way. The question is, is if you can change leadership style? Yes you can. But you'll have to go through a lot to change it.

Q: Is there a major flaw you see in leaders who have a large scandal or fail to reach their potential?

A: I would say infidelity.

Q: Why did you say that?

A: Infidelity is a huge scourge. When you cheat on your spouse, you cheat on God. It is a gigantic sin. And in politics, it's seen everywhere. I am a counselor who counsels politicians, and they are basically having affairs right and left. And I think it's a huge drag on their happiness, effectiveness, and on their life. People who have a genuinely good marriage tend to be great politicians. But there are very few people who do that. There are a lot of cheaters out there.

Q: What percentage of politicians would you say cheat on their spouses? I know you don't have stats in front of you, but give an estimate.

A: I would say way over 50%. 70% maybe.

Q: How does infidelity hurt a politician's effectiveness?

A: Well, first of all, they have to be dishonest. They have to have a secret second life and they have to lie about things. They can be easily manipulated. People can say, I know about your relationships, I want you to vote for my bill. There is just nothing good about an affair. I think what we're finding with technology in this country is that there will be fewer and fewer affairs.

Dr. Dayna Bowen Matthew: Dr. Matthew graduated from the University of Virginia Law School and also received a Degree in Economics from Harvard. As a writer, Dr. Matthew specializes in the legal arena and public health. As a professor, she's taught courses at the University of Colorado and the University of Virginia. Dr. Matthew's work also includes time serving as a Congressional Black Caucus Fellow, a Brookings Institute Fellow and Advisor to the Director of the Office of Civil Rights for the EPA. Early in her career, she appreciated coveted time clerking for Judge Thomas on the Virginia Supreme Court. Finally, Dr. Matthew has written a number of articles. Her book was published in 2015 and it is titled *Just Medicine*.

Q: Who helped form your character most?

A: My mother and my father. They were working-class African American people who came up from the south, to New York City during the Great Migration. My father and mother took hold of the American Dream like a cowboy takes hold of a bull with both hands. And they worked harder than any person I've met since to make sure that my brother and I left the South Bronx with the fullest range of opportunity for success in life–Marion and Vincent Bowen.

Q: What is your greatest achievement as a leader thus far?

A: Any student that I've taught and have been able to transfer values of equity, justice and compassion to would be my greatest achievement.

Q: You seem to be able to quite easily speak about uncomfortable topics. I would like to know how you do that. And if you don't feel completely comfortable talking about these intense topics

(healthcare & racial bias) what pushes you out of
your comfort zone to do that?

**A: As I have grown more senior in my field; I
have had the sense that I have a responsibility to
pay back the investment that's been made in me.
That pushes me out of my comfort zone. There
are people who depended and believed in me as
they gave me their best, even if it was a relatively
small investment. I went to a very large black
Baptist church growing up, and church was a big
part of my life. As I went to college and law
school, people in my church really believed I
could do something for a larger community.
Both of my parents died very young. My father
died when he was forty-nine and my mother died
when she was sixty-one. My father worked four
jobs at one point, and they stepped way out of
their comfort zone. They sent me to a
predominantly white school. I remember my
mother trembling when she had to go to parent-
teacher meetings. She did that with boldness in
order to make sure me and my brother got
opportunity. I've traveled widely, and I see more
injustice than I care to tolerate, so I've got to get
out of my comfort zone the way my mom and
dad did.**

Q: What are you reading outside of your work?

**A: Social science and scripture. I read biblical
books. Right now, I'm reading a book called**

Kingdom Calling, just to put my work into the context of God and what he's calling me to do. I love to read my children's writings. And I'm also reading about race relations and how things have come to be the way they are in the United States. And I'm also reading a book called *Whisper*, which my pastor wrote on how to hear the voice of God.

Q: What have you sacrificed in the past and what do you currently sacrifice to hold the leadership position you hold today?

A: My husband would say sleep (laughs). I have the sense that my family has paid a big price for me to work the way that I do. But I don't think I know or will know until I get to Heaven whether I successfully balanced it. For example, I came to D.C. in 2015 to get a more national perspective on healthcare policy. My husband and I still had a home in Colorado and we still worked in Colorado. He stayed in Colorado to work, so he sacrificed having a wife home every night so I could come to D.C. and rent an apartment and get tremendous experience at the EPA on Capitol Hill. We went into the hole. It paid off in increasing my leadership capacity, but my husband paid a big price.

Q: What was the reasoning behind leaving your job as a litigator? Someone could say that you could have made more money and had a greater impact on the system as a litigator.

A: My family. I did know I was having children and the schedule I was working as a litigator wasn't conducive to investing in them as my parents invested in me. The academic schedule is similar to my children's school schedule. They would have winter break and I would have winter break. It was a better fit for my family.

Q: You spent time in the political arena. What did you learn in your time there that has transferred over into the arena you work in now?

A: We all have power. Every single individual has power to influence the system for change.

Q: Why do you think character in leadership matters? There seems to be so many leaders that get by without it.

A: I'm not sure if I want to pass right now, because my thoughts are not clear. I'm very troubled by the misuse of the word character in the Christian Church. Character was supposed to count so much in the 70's, 80's and the 90's when Democrats were in power. The Christian Evangelical Church was so up in arms about Bill Clinton's character. But when faced with an African American family with high integrity and high character, they ran for the hills. And when faced with a candidate who was three times

married, misogynistic, racist and showed very low character, they've endorsed him at every opportunity. So, this phrase of character in leadership is a phrase that I feel very suspicious of. It doesn't matter to many people as much as outcome matters. As much as self-interest matters. I believe it does, but I don't believe it means anything with people who use that phrase often suggest.

Anne Miskey: Anne Miskey is the former CEO of the Downtown Women's Center. Currently, she serves as the CEO of Union Station Homeless Services. Mrs. Miskey's experience includes working with the Department of Housing and Urban Development and the Department of Veterans Affairs. She received a Bachelor's Degree from the University of Lethbridge and a Master of Divinity from the University of Toronto.

Q: Why did you choose to pursue a career in this field?

A: I worked many years in the corporate world after I got my Masters of Divinity Degree. I got that because I knew there was something in me that wanted to reach out, to help people, to work

with people. Being in the corporate world was not fulfilling to me, so I went into the non-profit world to make a difference. But what I was really looking to do in my career was not to do charitable work, but to actually look at how we make significant change in social issues.

Q: How do you focus on the mental state of homeless individuals? From the information and stats I've gathered, the vast majority of homeless individuals on Skid Row have a mental illness or have experienced traumatic events. What do you do to focus on their mental state?

A: We ask not what's wrong with you, but what's happened to you to put you in this situation. And that's a fundamental shift on how we deal with people when they walk in the door. The other piece of it is not how do we fix you, but how do we walk beside you in your journey as you become more and more empowered to build your life? How do we help people move to a place of healing? Whether its addiction, physical health issues, mental health issues or trauma. Most of the people we see are victims of extreme trauma. Sexual assault, domestic violence, child abuse, all of those things. It's probably more than 90% of the people we see.

Q: What are your strengths?

A: The ability to look at the big picture and the individual and bring them together. And I'm a good public speaker (laughs).

Q: What are you reading?

A: I've been reading a lot on social justice, equity and racism. I'm in a field that believes we do social justice well and we get diversity. Yet, I don't think we've really got to the heart of it. I understand that I am a privileged white woman; I don't understand a lot. I want to do the right thing and I don't always know what that is, so I'm struggling with that right now. Especially what's going on in this country right now.

Q: What is your greatest achievement as a leader thus far?

A: I feel like I'm on the journey still. Wow that's a tough one. I think, youth homelessness. I was a part of a group that changed the system about how we deal with youth homelessness. I also think I've helped change the conversation nationally about women's homelessness.

Q: What pitfalls have you tried to avoid?

A: Sometimes learning to say no to myself. I'm always excited about trying something new. You can overextend yourself personally and your staff. You can't be all things to all people. You have to stay on mission.

Q: How does your theological degree influence your decision-making?

A: It taught me really important lessons on how I approach things: the academics, looking at evidence and research. It can't just be based on feelings. A lot of people like to hand out food because it makes them feel good. Figure out how you can work on mercy as well as justice. Oh, and it taught me how to preach (laughs).

Q: How do you deal with pain?

A: I write really junky romance novels. The other thing that's important to me is to have a small group to talk to that knows what I'm dealing with. I don't work with them, but it's a group of CEOs. And I have a coach. She is a person that makes me feel uncomfortable and makes me grow.

Q: What is one attribute leaders need to have to lead in an excellent fashion?

A: Humility. Leadership can go to your head. Constantly learn and recognize that there are people around you that are better than you and smarter than you in lots of ways. And humor.

Q: Homelessness in Los Angeles grew by 23% last year. Knowing all you and your staff do, what is your mindset like after viewing those numbers? It can almost feel like defeat.

A: I think that affects us all. I think we need to celebrate the success. If all you see is the undone work on your desk, it's going to wear you down. If you look at the pile you finished, then you can balance it, and that's what we have to do. We have housed more than twice as many women as we housed last year. And over 95% of the women we house stay housed.

Q: Is there anything you would like to add on character in leadership?

A: Leadership is a privilege, and you can't deny that you get a lot out of it. It's nice being in charge. I like being in charge. We play ourselves false if we don't admit it. I decided a long time ago I didn't like working for other people. And it's funny, when I admitted to myself that that was okay, I started being a leader. Maybe, this being a woman thing, somehow it seemed wrong to be in charge. But no, that's a part of leadership. And again, not getting too big for your britches.

____

____

Secretary Leon Panetta: His illustrious career includes tenures as a former Chief of Staff for the President of the United States of America, former Director of the CIA, former Secretary of Defense, and former United States Congressman. His career also includes time in the United States Army, time as the Director of the Office of Civil Rights and experience as a litigator. Mr. Panetta co-founded the Panetta Institute for Public Policy with his wife Sylvia Panetta who is a star in her own right. Panetta was raised as a Catholic and served as an altar boy. He still carries a rosary to this day. Finally, Mr. Panetta has served on the Board of Directors for the New York Stock Exchange and has worked as a professor teaching at Santa Clara University.

Q: Why did you desire to become a politician?

A: My desire was to get involved in public service. I thought it was important to give back to the country. I am the son of immigrants. I served in the military and recognized that duty to country was extremely important. Then there was a young president that said, ask not what your country can do for you, but what you can do for your country. I looked at public service as a higher calling.

Q: What is your greatest achievement as a leader thus far?

A: I've enjoyed challenges in all of the public service positions I've had. In Congress, establishing the Monterey Bay National Marine

Sanctuary and helping establish CSU Monterey Bay. Providing Medicare benefits for hospice services. When I served as OMB Director and the President's Chief of Staff, the ability to develop tough budgets, that led to balanced budgets in the Federal Government and having a surplus was an accomplishment. In the CIA, doing the Bin Laden Operation. As Defense Secretary, the ability to develop new strategies for the twenty-first century, and lastly, the ability to open opportunities for everyone to serve in the military.

Q: What are your strengths?

A: I think I'm able to understand complex issues and weigh both sides. I think my law school education really prepared me well for public service. I'm able to understand different positions and try to find consensus. Determination, I do not take defeat easily and anytime I am defeated, I come back and fight that much harder. And compassion, feeling that the most important thing I can do is to try to help improve the lives of others. I feel that deeply and I believe it's an important quality to have.

Q: Other than yourself, who helped form your character most?

A: My Italian parents. They taught me to work hard, sacrifice, take risks and be willing to fight hard. Later in public life, I think the first U.S.

Senator I worked for, Thomas Kuchel, was a real inspiration for me because he taught me the importance of integrity–personal integrity, being honest with yourself and being honest with others.

Q: A few days ago, I was listening to former President Barack Obama speak with Bill and Melinda Gates. He said, 'Most politicians and elected leaders are followers and not leaders. They're called leaders, but most of the time they follow. They see what their constituents care about, then they respond.' My question to you is, how do you get out in front and take a proactive approach?

A: I think you have to be willing to take risks. You have to develop goals and listen to people. You have to be able to determine what goals can be achieved, then you have to make sure you are able to pursue those goals. Leadership by its very nature demands that you have to take risks. And if you're not willing to take a risks, you're not going to be a good leader. And I think that's what's lacking. Most elected officials are not willing to take the risk that they should be taking in order to solve problems.

Q: What pitfalls have you tried to avoid?

A: Compromising your sense of right and wrong for something you want to achieve. The toughest challenge is between your conscience and what's right and wrong. Whether or not you will be able

to enhance your career–that's a tough choice, but I think it's important to always choose what your conscience tells you.

Q: What is your mindset in a crisis?

A: Don't panic, keep a cool head and take a deep breath. Find out about the crisis, what steps need to be taken to resolve that crisis and make sure you can keep the country or your office on the right path.

Q: What have you sacrificed in the past and what do you currently sacrifice now to hold the leadership position you hold today?

A: The real challenge in public office are the demands that are placed on your family, especially when you have to travel to Washington and you have to deal with constituent needs. You have to make sure you set aside time for your family. The biggest sacrifice is absence from those you love.

____

____

Dr. Farnaz Tabaee: Born in Persia, Dr. Tabaee moved to the United States at the age of sixteen to escape war, attain a better life and step up to life's challenges. She attended a Catholic High School in New Jersey, worked hard to learn English and opened herself to a new religion and a nation of new laws. Dr. Tabaee's education includes a Degree in Electrical Engineering, a M.A. in Organizational Management and a Ph.D. in Educational Leadership from Pepperdine University. She's also ventured into Post-Doctorate work at the University of Florida. As a professor, Dr. Tabaee has taught classes at UCLA and California State University, Dominguez Hills. When she is not engaged in her work as a business consultant, Dr. Tabaee teaches classes on improv to budding actors.

Q: How do you deal with uncertainty as a leader?

A: Don't ignore new information or make impulsive decisions. Some leaders research a topic to death, then the opportunity passes. You have to learn how to navigate change and be okay with failure. Failure is just data. When you go to the circus and someone falls, what do they do? They get up and celebrate it. I teach people to celebrate their failures. There is no other way to learn. There is no shortcut.

Q: How do you build a team, how do you keep a cool head, and how do you make good decisions under pressure?

A: I think improv can do that. Improv is acting without a script, but there are boundaries that you have to follow in improv. Improv actors

have to say, "yes and" as a response to any sort of communication. This makes you really listen to people, deep listening. Then you allow them to influence you. You allow them to change you.

Q: How does that transfer over to business?

A: If you do improv all the time, you will stop micromanaging people and controlling people. You speak more authentically instead of being in the future or past or being scared. For improv to work, you have to listen to one another. Another rule of improv is that you have to work to make your partner look good. Status is equal in improv. In business, it doesn't matter if it's your boss or the janitor. This allows people to speak up. It builds character, teams and a form of collaboration that you don't typically see in business. It's different than sports; in sports you have a team, but there is always a hero. There is no hero in improv. People who can't do improv are the ones who want a lot of attention or can't give away their power.

Q: What do you mean by that? "That they don't want to give away their power."

A: You don't have any power in improv. You have to be in the moment. It's a bit hard to explain if you don't actually do it.

Q: What is your greatest achievement as a leader thus far?

A: As a consultant, helping companies. I have always kept my integrity and authenticity while helping them be more effective. I haven't taken jobs that I know are unethical. A company might want me to take a job to cover for firing somebody.

Q: How do you refrain from taking a job when you may receive personal funding or a promotion in your career?

A: I sleep better at night. That's why I don't take those kinds of jobs. It's empathy. I put myself in the position of the person I'm affecting. I think it's the empathy. Money has never been my goal in business.

Q: So, what's the goal?

A: The goal is to help people. That is my number one goal in business. And if I can't help them, I don't take the job or I refer them to somebody else. The job I told you about, I left that job. I burned bridges, I left the company, but that's okay. Who wants to work for somebody like that? Who wants a reference from somebody like that?

Q: What are you reading right now outside of your work?

A: *Loyalty to Your Soul*. It talks about integrity and how to be more authentic in your life. It teaches you how to provide service.

<u>Rebecca Walton:</u> (Young Leader)

Born in Australia, Rebecca Walton currently serves as a Director for Global Tribe. Global Tribe is a non-profit that organizes and performs service missions to countries in Africa. Rebecca's passion for disadvantaged communities began in her early years. While studying in high school and college, Rebecca took numerous trips to the slums of Mexico. On occasion, she brought a team of workers with her and they began to organize projects collectively. Her undertakings included building houses, schools, churches and orphanage dormitories. In Africa, Mrs. Walton launched a group savings and loan program. The project has fourteen savings groups with over one hundred and fifty women enrolled. Rebecca received a degree in Business Studies in New Zealand. In addition to her service mission history, she worked for four years as a finance analyst, business analyst and software project manager.

Q: One word or phrase that describes the mental attitude you try to maintain during difficult situations?

A: Accept and move forward.

Q: What are your strengths?

A: Positivity and having the ability to get things done.

Q: What have you sacrificed in the past, and what do you currently sacrifice now to hold the leadership position you hold today?

A: I sacrificed my time and salary when I moved to Africa. I did not have a salary waiting for me, but a few people supported me during my trip. There were language barriers in Kenya, theft, corruption of all kinds, and I even contracted malaria during my stay. People here in America complain about small things. They complain about cell service, having to wait in the queue (line) or even their jobs. It's really not that big of a deal.

Q: What motivates you to help the people in Kenya? Someone might say, why not help here in America, there are people who need help here, why would you go over there?

A: I went to Kenya when I was nineteen. I took a gap year off from school. As I toured Africa, my desire to help the people grew. I saw people in remote areas that seemed isolated and almost helpless. I wanted to give back. People ask me that all the time, but there are a lot of support systems in LA. There are people here giving back.

Q: What attribute do leaders need to possess to lead others in an excellent fashion?

A: Trust. You need to place trust in your followers.

Q: What leadership mistakes have you made in the past?

A: Jumping to conclusions, being impatient, and being a control freak. I'm a perfectionist and wanting to be perfect prevents me from getting things done sometimes.

<u>Bibliography:</u>

<u>Chapter 2</u>

1.History of B-CU.
www.cookman.edu/about_bcu/history/

2.Bevely Johnson-Miller. Mary McLeod
Bethune.http://www.talbot.edu/ce20/educators/prote
stant/mary_bethune/

<u>Chapter 6</u>

1.Sophie Haigney. 24 Hour Fitness settles claims it
misled gym members with rates.
https://www.sfchronicle.com/business/article/24-
Hour-Fitness-settles-claims-it-misled-gym-
12327376.php. 11-2-2017

About the Author:

Barry Heads II is a leader still working on his character. His education includes a degree in Political Science from California State University, Fresno and the pursuit of a Master's of Divinity from Gateway Seminary.

In addition to educational pursuits, Barry's work history includes working for the United States Congress, United States Attorney's Office, the State of California and the University of Southern California.

Barry resides in Southern California and is an avid fan of writing. He enjoys public speaking and engaging in local church activities.

From the Author:

Don't Become the Marine Biologist!